# FRENCH
## COOKING

## THE GREAT
## TRADITIONAL RECIPES

**EB BONECHI**

## HOW TO READ THE CARDS

| DIFFICULTY | FLAVOUR | NUTRITIONAL CONTENT |
|---|---|---|
| ● Easy | ● Mild | ● Low |
| ●● Medium | ●● Medium | ●● Medium |
| ●●● Difficult | ●●● Strong | ●●● High |

Preparation and cooking times are shown in hours (h) and minutes (e. g. 30' is 30 minutes).

Most of these recipes, especially where the preparation is more complex, are illustrated by photo sequences to make them easier to follow. We advise you, before starting, to carefully run through the list of ingredients (where you will also find the preparation and cooking times, an indication of the degree of difficulty and of the strength of flavour, and a breakdown of the nutritional values). You should then read through the various steps of the recipe with care, after which, all that remains is for us to wish you Bon Appétit!

NOTES AND SUGGESTIONS TO READERS:
In the text oven temperatures are given in centigrade. The following conversion chart may be useful:

150 °C/ 300 °F/ GAS MARK 2
160 °C/ 325 °F/ GAS MARK 3
175 °C/ 350 °F/ GAS MARK 4
190 °C/ 375 °F/ GAS MARK 5
200 °C/ 400 °F/ GAS MARK 6
220 °C/ 425 °F/ GAS MARK 7
230 °C/ 450 °F/ GAS MARK 8

*Project:* Casa Editrice Bonechi
*Series editor:* Alberto Andreini
*Concept and Coordination:* Paolo Piazzesi
*Graphic design:* Andrea Agnorelli and Maria Rosanna Malagrinò
*Cover and make-up:* Maria Rosanna Malagrinò
*Editing:* Patrizia Chirichigno

*Translation:* Aelmuire Helen Cleary

*Chef:* Lisa Mugnai
*Dietician:* Dr. John Luke Hili

*The photographs of the food are the property of the* Casa Editrice Bonechi *Archives and were taken by* Andrea Fantauzzo

*The scenic photographs, property of the* Casa Editrice Bonechi *Archives, were taken by:*
Paolo Giambone (pp. 3 top, 4 top, 5 top, 6, 32, 38, 50, 74, 87, 90, 100, 120),
Gianni Dagli Orti (pp. 5 bottom, 8, 124),
Luigi Di Giovine (pp. 16, 92, 112), Jean-Charles Pinheira (pp. 13, 54, 114),
Andrea Pistolesi (pp. 3 bottom, 4 bottom, 44)

*Other collaborators include:* J. Bonnet-Beaulieu (p. 84),
Maurizio Fraschetti (p. 52), Otus (p. 49)

*For the photographs with no identified source,
the Publisher would appreciate any information so as to integrate reprinted editions.*

© *by* CASA EDITRICE BONECHI, Firenze - Italia
*E-mail: bonechi@bonechi.it    Internet: www.bonechi.it - www.bonechi.com*

*Printed in Italy by* Centro Stampa Editoriale Bonechi, *Sesto Fiorentino (Firenze)*

*The cover, layout and artworks by the* Casa Editrice Bonechi *graphic artists
in this publication, are protected by international copyright.*

ISBN 978-88-476-0876-4

A 10 9 8 7 6 5 4 3 2 1

# A GASTRONOMIC TOUR OF FRANCE

*Soupe à l'oignon, Escargots à la bourguignonne, Quiche lorraine, Tarte Tatin*: all over the world, the very mention of these dishes immediately evokes the flavour of France. These are among the many recipes you will find in this book, alongside others which are perhaps less famous, at least outside their regions of origin, but no less delicious and characteristic. And so we invite you to accompany us on this rather special treasure hunt to unearth the myriad treasures of the land of the Tricolour. It is a voyage of discovery through an exceptional heritage, deserving of respect and conservation, which in its expansive variety faithfully reflects the multi-faceted nature of the country, representing at the same time a potent antidote to the current tendency towards a standardisation of taste.

*Two views of Paris. Above: the equestrian monument to Henri IV on the Pont-Neuf. Below: a chariot adorning the Grand Palais.*

As well as featuring significantly in the national budget, the treasures which France offers us open-handed – meat, poultry, sausages and salamis, pâtés, cheeses, conserves, cakes and pastries, wines and liqueurs – are not just gastronomic delights but distinctive features of the national culture. This is a culture which is authentic and vital, and which makes each village, each small restaurant, each local *charcutier* a discovery and an unforgettable experience, an adventure in the enchanted realm of flavour.

Our journey begins on the broad plains overlooking the North Sea: the wonderful fish of Boulogne-sur-Mer, the leading fishing port of France, is the prime ingredient of the excellent *Caudière de Berck*. Then we come to Flanders, where beer predominates over wine and is combined with the fine butter to offer us delights such as *Goyère, Carbonnade* (or *Carbonade*), *Potjevleisch* and *Asperges à la flamande*. Neighbouring Picardy replies with the famous *Caghuse* (or *Caqhuse*) and the *Tarte à l'Badrée*.

While Paris, a veritable Babel of gastronomic languages, tempts us with an infinite range of delicacies which reaches the sublime it its matchless confectionery (we have only to think of the *Saint-Honoré*), in the hinterland of the capital the Île-de-France entices us with splendid cheeses and luscious vegetables.

And so we come to Normandy – a land of marked contrasts which are reflected in a varied and generous gastronomy, rich in simple, flavoursome dishes – which boasts one of the major French cookery schools. This is the country of fine milk and fabulous cheeses (*camembert, livarot, pont-l'évêque* and *neufchâtel* to mention but a few), and of the famous *agneau de pré-salé* or saltmarsh lamb with its inimitable flavour, due to the fact that the animals graze in coastal pastures rich in salt and iodine. It is the land of apples and fine cider, of Calvados and Bénédictine, but most of all it is the realm of marine delicacies, with a wealth of fish, crustaceans and molluscs, starting with the exquisite oysters of Courseulles-sur-Mer and Saint-Vaast-la-Hougue. Among the tempting range of Norman delights, we have selected *Épaule d'agneau au chou, Jambonneaux au cidre, Poulet au cidre et aux carottes de Créances, Huîtres au gratin, Turbot braisé au cidre, Pommes de terre à la normande* and to round off *Bourdelots* and *Tergoule* (or *Teurgoule*).

To define Brittany as the ardent rival of Normandy would be reductive, even if, effectively, here too we find milk and milk products,

*Paris: an old shop-sign in the Marais and, below, the statue of Victory which crowns the Châtelet fountain.*

saltmarsh lamb, cider and an extensive assortment of fish, molluscs and crustaceans, with the famous oysters of Auray, Belon and Cancale, the delicate *Coquilles Saint-Jacques*, the lobsters from Camaret on the Crozon peninsula, and a shimmering wealth of bass, cod, dorado, turbot and tuna. The essential cuisine – spontaneous and rustic – of the regions of Armor and Arcoat in the western extremity of France betwixt ocean and forest, has a distinctively marked personality, not least because of the use of exotic buckwheat in the *far* or batter pudding, and that of spices such as curry, pepper and Cayenne pepper, originally brought by the slave-ships that put into port at Nantes. The choice examples of Breton cooking we propose include: *Friands de Douarnenez, Gigot d'agneau à la bretonne, Bardatte*, a typical harvest-time dish, *Poulet aux oignons et far, Calmars à l'armoricaine, Haricots à la bretonne, Far aux pruneaux*, and *Kouign-aman* (or *Kuign amann*). A whiff of Breton cooking is also to be caught in the region of Nantes, the land of the master fish-salters, through which we proceed to the delights of the cuisine of the Loire, rich in choice vegetables (*Gratin de blettes*), and famous for its goat's milk cheeses and its furred and feathered game. After the sea fish (*Daurade aux cèpes*) here we also have the freshwater varieties (*Ragoût d'anguilles et de cuisses de grenouille*), protagonists of a cuisine where wine is generously used, especially in the poultry-based dishes (*Canard nantais rôti dans son jus au muscadet*), finishing up with a delicious *Tarte solognate aux épices*.

We proceed through Aunis and the Charente, with a coastline offering superb oysters, and without neglecting to taste the exquisite *Chaudrée saintongeaise*, savouring the cooking of the Bordeaux region which makes wide use of its famous wines. This is a flavoursome, aromatic cuisine which focuses on cheeses, and to an even greater degree, on meats both red and white, game, mushrooms and the fish from the Gironde estuary.

We move on into the Pays Basque, where in the kitchen French is spoken with a Spanish accent: spicy and peppery as in the piment rouge of Espelette and the piment vert of Anglet (*Rouzole, Hachua* or *Achoa, Jarret de porc aux épices, Poulet à la mode de Sare*), delicate in the superb Bayonne ham, produced from pigs which feed in the oak and chestnut woods, as bracing as the sea air (*Chipirons farcis, Thon basquais*), or as sweet and soothing as the *Milhassou*.

While Béarn regales us with the robust and aromatic *Garbure*, a meal in itself, the savour of truffles awaits us in Périgord, the land of *foie gras* and *confit*, where as well as game, the woods yield up delicious mushrooms. In a region famed for its culinary traditions, everyday cooking, which is strictly based on local produce, is transformed into top quality gastronomy: you have only to try the *Soupe de campagne ou des vendangeurs*, the *Enchaud*, the *Pommes sarladaises* or the *Cajassé de Sarlat*. And so we come to another famous wine region, also renowned for its *marcs* and its *raisiné*. Here the culture of the grape, which has its roots in the wine-making traditions of the ancient monastic complexes such as the famous Abbey of Cluny, is matched by an equally exquisite gastronomic culture which dates back to the period when the ducal court resided in Dijon, homeland of the excellent mustard. Burgundy, the fertile land of vines and pastures, of fine sausages and cheeses such as *Charolais*, tempts us with a generous cuisine which as well as delighting the palate, also cheers the heart. Here our proposals include *Œufs en meurette, Escargots de Bourgogne*, the triumphal *Bœuf bourguignon* (made using exclusively the tasty meat from the healthy herds of Charolais), *Écrevisses au gratin* and the delicious dessert *Piqueuchâgne*. In nearby Champagne, synonymous with the most famous spumante wines in the world, we can enjoy *Parmentier d'agneau, Pigeons en marinade* and, from the richly-stocked rivers, *Perche aux noix*.

Serenely impartial Lorraine, where German influence blends with French sagacity, makes no distinction between its superb wine and excellent beer. The variety of the landscape, with its pastures and forests, lakes and rivers, is also reflected in the produce, including an excellent smoked ham, and in the cooking. Here, alongside the world-famous *Quiche lorraine*, originally made without bacon, we can also savour the *Potée lorraine* and the sophisticated *Cailles de Stanislas*. The peaceful co-existence of wine and beer is also the rule in neighbouring Alsace, homeland of the *choucroute*. This famous dish of chopped, salted cabbage seasoned with bay leaf and juniper and stewed in wine, would be enough in itself to ensure undying fame to a cuisine which also claims the merit of having invented the *foie gras*. But the refined culinary tradition of Alsace is also justly renowned for its robust and nourishing soups, its preserved meats, its veal, game and poultry, especially the stuffed goose which is traditionally eaten during the Christmas celebrations. As well as smoked herrings, freshwater fish also abound, like the salmon and trout from the Rhine. Among the most famous Alsace dishes, which once again illustrate how the traditions of rural cooking have evolved into a sophisticated school of gastronomy, we propose: *Fricandeau*, *Bäckeofe* (or *Bäckeoffe* or again *Baekenofe*) of relatively recent origin, *Flammekueche* (or *Flammenküche*) and fish-based recipes, both robust such as the *Matelote à l'alsacienne*, and more delicate such as *Truites au Riesling*, accompanied by *Pommes de terre farcies* and rounded off by a splendid *Kougelhopf*.

The region of Lyons vies with Burgundy for the supremacy of regional cooking, boosted by the contribution of the splendid wines of Beaujolais and the Côtes du Rhône. Traditionally a gourmet's city, Lyons boasts a simple cuisine inspired by ancient folk wisdom set at the service of the great masters of modern French cooking. Particularly famous are the poultry from the pond-rich area of Bresse, the cheeses of the Drôme, *Saint-marcellin* and *Mont-d'or*, the pike and carp from the ponds of the Dombes, the vegetables, starring the best chard in the world, and the fruit, including the famous *marrons*, and above all the superfine sausages and preserved meats. Exceptional among these are the *saucisson de Lyon*, either normal or with pistachio or truffle, the *cervelas* (which is now no longer made with brain) and the *saucisson à cuire*. If Paris is the international culinary me-

tropolis, Lyons, *"ville de gueule"*, is without doubt the gastronomic capital of France. It matches the bistrots of the former with its *bouchons*, where it is de rigueur

*A corner of one of the most characteristic cities of Provence: L'Isle-sur-la-Sorgue; below, the elegant dining-room in the Castle of Anet.*

to try the *mâchon* filled with sausage, or to savour the *tablier de sapeur*. From the laden table of the Lyons area we have selected the *Soupe à l'oignon*, brought back to fashion by Paul Bocuse, the *Gâteau de foies de volaille*, the *Pintade au chou*, the *Saladier lyonnais* and, for the sweet final note, the apple *Matefaim*.

Nearby Savoy, with its rivers and lakes abounding in fish, also boasts a tradition of superb cheeses, such as *Abondance*, *Beaufort* and *Reblochon*, of a fame only matched by that of its

confectionery. Here we are regaled by the tempting flavours of *Crique de Savoie*, *Morue à la crème* and *Truites à la mode*.

An unmistakable aroma of herbs and garlic heralds our arrival in the region of the sun-drenched cuisine of Nice and Provence. Inviting, light and appetising, as well as boasting a host of famous local specialities to be accompanied by the exceptional regional wines, this is a type of cooking which is also to be recommended from a dietary point of view because of the

*The entrance to one of the Paris Métro stations, designed in the early twentieth century.*

almost exclusive use of olive oil. After the aromatic sauces, from *Aïoli* to *Tapenade*, which are an ideal accompaniment for the exquisite Mediterranean fish, you should also try the *Œufs en berlingueto*, the famous Marseilles *Bouillabaisse* and the basil-scented *Soupe au pistou*, to be followed by *Bœuf en daube*, *Lapin provençal*, *Morue en raïto*, *Poulpes en daube*, *Thon à la provençale*, *Artichauts à la barigoule* and the *Ratatouille niçoise*.

Another superbly felicitous combination of land and sea also characterises the fragrant cuisine of Languedoc, where the robust bean-based *Cassoulet* harmonises perfectly with the delicate fish dishes.

In Roussillon, with its sweet Muscat wines, the language in the kitchen is Catalan and we are tempted by excellent salamis such as *Gambajo* and *Boutifarra*, as well as by gleaming fresh anchovies and sardines. Here, justly exhausted at the end of our Grand Tour, we will sit down with pleasure to enjoy the *Aïgo boulido*, *Soupe bourgeoise à la sétoise* or *Soupe de moules comme au Grau-du-roi*, the traditional Camargue *Gardianne* (or *Gardiane*), *Lotte en bourride*, *Tiella* and the supremely Catalan *Crema cremada* (or *cramada*).

# DIETICIAN'S ADVICE

*T*he dietetics of French cooking is a perfect example of how European gastronomy varies on the basis of latitude. The cuisine of Provence and the Midi is very similar to the Mediterranean diet, while that of Normandy, Brittany and Alsace is more closely related to the Anglo-Saxon and Germanic tradition, and then we must make due exception for the "nordic" type diet of the Alpine regions and Savoy. In the Midi vegetable condiments are favoured, in particular olive oil; the carbohydrates tend to originate from wheat and its derivatives, and vegetables are abundantly used. The result is a type of cuisine very similar to the Mediterranean diet, with the lion's share represented by complex carbohydrates (55-60% of the daily calorie intake), while the use of olive oil means that the lipids are prevalently monounsaturates, and vegetable fibres abound. In the north of the country animal fats (butter, lard, bacon fat) are more widely used (35-40%), while the complex carbohydrates (45-50%) are mostly supplied by potatoes. It is by now common knowledge that generally the Mediterranean-type diet is to be preferred, since the components tend to prevent the development of arterial sclerosis. Naturally, the occasional enjoyment of some of the marvellous dishes from Breton or Alsace illustrated in this book presents absolutely no risk to health, in spite of the dietician's critique; the important thing is not to cultivate the habit of an over-rich diet.

# INDEX OF RECIPES

*A view of Nice, one of the most famous cities
of the Côte d'Azur.*

# LES ENTRÉES

*First courses to get the meal off to a delicious start.
Inspired ideas for light lunches or suppers,
accompanied by vegetables or salad.
Perfect for hors d'œuvres and snacks.*

1

500 g/ 1 lb 2 oz potatoes
2 eggs
1 large Spanish onion
1 bunch chives
Nutmeg
60 g/ 2 oz butter
12 slices raw Savoy or Parma
   ham (to accompany)
Salt and pepper

| | |
|---|---|
| Servings: 4 | |
| Preparation time: 30' | |
| Cooking time: about 30' | |
| Difficulty: ● | |
| Flavour: ● ● | |
| Kcal (per serving): 372 | |
| Proteins (per serving): 8 | |
| Fats (per serving): 29 | |
| Nutritional value: ● ● ● | |

# CRIQUE DE SAVOIE

Potato cakes ☛ *Savoy*

P eel and grate the potatoes, slice the onion very fine and chop the chives. In a large bowl, beat the eggs and mix in the grated potatoes, the onion and the chives. Season with salt and pepper and add a pinch of grated nutmeg. Shape with your hands into four flattened cakes, then heat the butter in a frying-pan and fry for 5 to 7 minutes on each side.
Serve hot, accompanied with the sliced ham and a green salad.

# ESCARGOTS EN PAUPIETTES DE CHOU

**Snail rolls ☛ *Burgundy***

1 Remove the outer leaves of the cabbage, and scald about thirty of the inner leaves in salted water, with the two unpeeled cloves of garlic, for 3 minutes.
Lift out the cabbage leaves with a slatted spoon; let the garlic cook for a further 2 minutes, then remove and set aside.

2 Clean and chop the shallots, then sauté in a knob of butter. Lay the scalded cabbage leaves on a marble work-surface, sprinkle over the chopped shallots, place a snail in the centre of each and roll up. Heat the chicken stock over a gentle heat; carefully drop in the snail rolls to warm them through, then place 7 in each serving bowl.
Raise the heat to reduce the chicken stock, then add the mashed garlic, the chopped herbs and the second knob of butter. Season with salt and pepper to taste, pour the sauce over the snail rolls, and serve.

28 snails (jarred)
1 Savoy cabbage
2 cloves garlic
4 shallots
1/4 litre/8 fl oz/ 1 cup chicken stock
2 knobs butter
2 tablespoons chopped herbs (chives, tarragon, chervil and parsley)
Salt and pepper

| | |
|---|---|
| Servings: | 4 |
| Preparation time: | 30′ |
| Cooking time: | 15′ |
| Difficulty: | ● ● |
| Flavour: | ● ● |
| Kcal (per serving): | 303 |
| Proteins (per serving): | 24 |
| Fats (per serving): | 15 |
| Nutritional value: | ● |

# FLAMMEKUECHE

Flat onion bread ☞*Alsace*

500 g/ 1 lb 2 oz bread dough
200 ml/ 6 fl oz/ ³/₄ cup
  single cream
50 g/2 oz onion
80 g/ 3 oz smoked bacon
50 g/ 2 oz butter
Nutmeg
Olive oil
Salt and pepper

| | |
|---|---|
| Servings: 4 | |
| Preparation time: 20' | |
| Cooking time: 15' | |
| Difficulty: ● ● | |
| Flavour: ● ● ● | |
| Kcal (per serving): 695 | |
| Proteins (per serving): 9 | |
| Fats (per serving): 49 | |
| Nutritional value: ● ● ● | |

Roll out the bread dough thin and lay it on an oiled baking tray. Clean and chop the onion and sauté gently in the butter, then tip it into a bowl, mix with the cream and season with salt, pepper and a pinch of grated nutmeg. Scald the bacon in boiling salted water (5 minutes), then dice. Cover the bread dough with the onion and cream mixture, then scatter over the diced bacon. Bake for ten minutes in a pre-heated oven at maximum heat.

# FRIANDS DE DOUARNENEZ

Sardine puffs ☞ *Brittany*

Cook the sardines in the butter for two minutes each side. Roll out the puff pastry to a thickness of 3 mm/ 1/8 in and cut into 12 rectangles of 5 x 12 cm/2 x 5 in. Fillet the sardines, removing the heads, tails and bones, which will give you 12 fillets. Place one at the side of each rectangle, then roll up the pastry and seal the edges well with your fingertips. Place the sardine puffs on a baking tray slightly moistened with water, brush with the egg yolk beaten with a little water, then bake in a pre-heated oven at 200°C for a quarter of an hour.

*The reefs of the Crozon peninsula in Brittany.*

6 fresh sardines, cleaned
250 g/ 9 oz puff pastry
20 g/ 2/3 oz butter
1 egg yolk

| | |
|---|---|
| Servings: 4 | |
| Preparation time: 30′ | |
| Cooking time: 20′ | |
| Difficulty: ● ● | |
| Flavour: ● ● ● | |
| Kcal (per serving): 566 | |
| Proteins (per serving): 10 | |
| Fats (per serving): 45 | |
| Nutritional value: ● ● ● | |

# GOUGÈRES

## Cheese choux puffs ☞ *Burgundy*

1/4 litre/ 1/2 pint/ 1 cup milk
100 g/ 3 1/2 oz butter
150 g/ 5 oz flour
4 eggs and 1 yolk
50 g/ 2 oz Gruyère cheese,
    finely diced
Salt

| | |
|---|---|
| **Servings:** 4 | |
| **Preparation time:** 25' | |
| **Cooking time:** 25' | |
| **Difficulty:** ● ● | |
| **Flavour:** ● ● | |
| **Kcal (per serving):** 1097 | |
| **Proteins (per serving):** 60 | |
| **Fats (per serving):** 77 | |
| **Nutritional value:** ● ● ● | |

**1** Put the milk and the butter in a saucepan with a pinch of salt and bring to the boil. Fold in the flour and continue cooking, stirring all the time, for 5 minutes until the mixture begins to come away from the edges of the pan. Leave to cool, then add the eggs one by one, and the diced cheese.

Mix thoroughly until you have a smooth paste.

**2** Roll the mixture into small balls, brush with the beaten egg yolk and set them in a fairly flat, buttered ovenproof dish. Cook in a pre-heated oven at 180°C for 20 minutes.

**1**

**2**

# GOYÈRE

Savoury cheese tart ☞ *Hainaut and Flanders*

Dilute the yeast in a drop of warm water, and stir in the sugar; add a tablespoon of flour to the warm beer. Tip the rest of the flour into a large bowl and add the salt, the eggs, the softened butter, the yeast and the beer. Work the ingredients thoroughly together until you have a smooth, pliable dough, then roll out and line a buttered and floured flan dish. Cover with a clean tea-cloth, and leave to rise in a warm place for an hour.

Remove the rind from the cheese, mash it up with a fork and blend in the eggs, the other soft cheese, the cream, flour, salt and pepper. Tip this mixture into the dough-lined flan dish and bake in a pre-heated oven at 210°C for 25-30 minutes.

*For the dough:*
250 g/ 9 oz flour
15 g/ 1/2 oz fresh yeast
4 tablespoons of beer
1 teaspoon muscovado,
  or other brown sugar
2 eggs
100 g/ 3 1/2 oz butter
1/2 teaspoon salt

*For the filling:*
300 g/ 11 oz Maroilles
  cows' cheese
250 g/ 9 oz soft, fresh,
  Sahnequark-type cheese
3 tablespoons double
  or cooking cream
2 eggs
20 g/ 2/3 oz butter
15 g/ 1/2 oz flour
Salt and pepper

| | |
|---|---|
| Servings: 6-8 | |
| Preparation time: 30' + 1 h | |
| Cooking time: 30' | |
| Difficulty: ● ● ● | |
| Flavour: ● ● | |
| Kcal (per serving): 591 | |
| Proteins (per serving): 27 | |
| Fats (per serving): 40 | |
| Nutritional value: ● ● ● | |

*Maroilles (Appellation d'Origine protegée) is a soft cheese, often square-shaped, pale yellow in colour and slightly elastic in consistency, with a distinctly strong flavour and smell. The rind is red and rough; the maturing of the cheese lasts for six months during which time it is subjected to frequent immersions in brine.*

# ŒUFS EN BERLINGUETO

## Stuffed eggs ☞ *Provence*

8 eggs
6 salted anchovies
2 slices stale bread
2 cloves garlic
2 egg yolks
150 ml/ 5 fl oz/ ¹/₂ cup
  single cream
Breadcrumbs
Parsley, basil
Olive oil
Salt and pepper

| | |
|---|---|
| Servings: 4 | |
| Preparation time: 15' | |
| Cooking time: 20' | |
| Difficulty: ● | |
| Flavour: ● ● ● | |
| Kcal (per serving): 886 | |
| Proteins (per serving): 37 | |
| Fats (per serving): 56 | |
| Nutritional value: ● ● ● | |

1 Soak the bread in the cream. Boil the eggs for 7 minutes, then shell them and cut in half. Scoop out the yolks and tip into the blender.
Rinse, bone and fillet the anchovies, then put them in the blender too, along with a sprig each of parsley and basil, the peeled garlic and the bread, with the excess cream squeezed out (keeping this aside).Whiz gently until you have a smooth paste.

*The castle overlooking the village of Le Barroux in Provence.*

2 Tip the mixture into a bowl and blend in the raw egg yolks with a pinch of salt and pepper. Stuff the boiled eggs with this mixture, and arrange in an oiled ovenproof dish, then sprinkle with breadcrumbs a trickle over the leftover cream. Ba in a pre-heated oven at 190-20C for 10 minutes. Excellent as an *h d'œuvre* or a buffet dish.

# ŒUFS EN MEURETTE

Eggs in wine ☞ *Burgundy*

8 eggs
100 g/ 3 1/2 oz unsmoked
  fatty bacon (in one piece)
1/2 bottle red wine
20 g/ 2/3 oz butter
20 g/ 2/3 oz flour
1 onion
3 shallots
1 bouquet garni (parsley,
  tarragon, thyme)
Slices of baguette, rubbed
  with garlic
Salt and pepper

| | |
|---|---|
| Servings: 4 | |
| Preparation time: 20' | |
| Cooking time: 1 h | |
| Difficulty: ● ● | |
| Flavour: ● ● ● | |
| Kcal (per serving): 490 | |
| Proteins (per serving): 26 | |
| Fats (per serving): 24 | |
| Nutritional value: ● ● | |

Melt the butter in a saucepan over a low heat, add the flour and blend it in smoothly, letting it colour but not brown. Add the chopped bacon and pour in the wine, a scant 100 ml/ 3 1/2 fl oz/ 1/2 cup of water, the chopped onion and shallots and the bouquet garni; season with salt and pepper and simmer slowly for a good half hour. Sieve the sauce, removing the bouquet garni, and fill four individual ovenproof dishes two-thirds full; break two eggs carefully into each, then bake in a pre-heated oven at 200°C removing while the yolks are still liquid. Season with freshly-ground pepper and serve with the slices of bread rubbed with garlic.

# QUICHE LORRAINE

*☛ Lorraine*

1 Prepare the pastry (see below) then set in the fridge to chill. Cut the bacon into thin strips and sauté in a frying-pan in 30 g/ 1 oz melted butter.

2 Keeping the whites to one side, blend the four egg yolks with the flour in a bowl, using either a whisk or the food processor.

3 Mix in the cream, a little at a time, adding a pinch of salt and pepper, and a sprinkle of grated nutmeg if desired.

4 Roll out the pastry and line a buttered flan dish, then spread the sautéed bacon and the diced cheese over the base. Beat the egg whites stiffly, fold them delicately into the quiche mixture, then pour into the pastry case. Bake in a pre-heated oven at 180°C for about 30 minutes. 5-6 minutes before the time is up, remove and brush with the beaten egg yolk, then return to the oven.

## BRISÉE PASTRY
PREPARATION TIME: 20'+ 45';
COOKING TIME: 10-15'; SERVINGS: 6

INGREDIENTS: 300 g/ 11 oz flour; 150 g/ 5 ½ oz butter; 1 egg yolk; a scant 100 ml/ 3 ½ fl oz/ ½ cup of milk; salt.

*In a bowl, cut the softened butter into flakes and blend it with the egg yolk and a pinch of salt. Tip in the flour, and rub it in with your fingertips, gradually adding a few drops of warm milk to lighten the dough. Roll into a ball, dust with flour, wrap in a clean tea-cloth and set to chill in the fridge for about half an hour. After this, roll it out not too thin and fold in two to form a small loaf shape, which you should chill again for fifteen minutes. After this the pastry is ready to roll out and use. Since in brisée pastry the proportion of butter to flour is of one to two, if you need to adjust the quantity of flour, that of the butter should be modified accordingly.*

Brisée pastry (see facing page)
200 g/ 7 oz smoked
  fatty bacon
150 g/ 5 oz Gruyère cheese
50 g/ 2 oz flour
200 ml/ 6 fl oz/ 3/4 cup cream
4 eggs + 1 yolk
Nutmeg (optional)

60 g/ 2 oz butter
Salt and pepper

| | |
|---|---|
| Servings: | 4-6 |
| Preparation time: | 35'+ 45' |
| Cooking time: | 40' |
| Difficulty: | ● ● ● |
| Flavour: | ● ● |
| Kcal (per serving): | 1229 |
| Proteins (per serving): | 26 |
| Fats (per serving): | 99 |
| Nutritional value: | ● ● ● |

# ROUZOLE

## Bacon and ham pancake ☞ *Ariégeois (Toulouse region)*

150 g/ 5 oz sliced fatty
 bacon
150 g/ 5 oz raw ham
3 eggs
1 slice bread (crumb only)
2 cloves garlic
2 leaves mint
15 g/ ¹/₂ oz lard (or butter)

| | |
|---|---|
| Servings: 4 | |
| Preparation time: 15' | |
| Cooking time: 20' | |
| Difficulty: ● | |
| Flavour: ● ● ● | |
| Kcal (per serving): 838 | |
| Proteins (per serving): 20 | |
| Fats (per serving): 66 | |
| Nutritional value: ● ● ● | |

Chop the bacon and the ham finely, then tip into a bowl with the beaten eggs. Add the bread crumb, the finely-chopped garlic and the crumbled mint leaves. Form into a pancake and brown in a frying-pan lightly greased with lard or butter. Ten minutes each side are more than sufficient.

# LES SOUPES

*From the coast, from the countryside and from the city; soups to start off the meal, or even as a light meal in themselves - allowing us to indulge in a rich dessert.*

2

# AÏGO BOULIDO

Garlic soup ☛ *Languedoc*

1 head garlic
4 slices stale white bread
Mature pecorino (sheep's)
   cheese, not too salty
Bay leaf and sage
Olive oil
Salt and pepper

| | |
|---|---|
| Servings: 4 | |
| Preparation time: 15' | |
| Cooking time: 20' | |
| Difficulty: ● ● | |
| Flavour: ● ● ● | |
| Kcal (per serving): 442 | |
| Proteins (per serving): 12 | |
| Fats (per serving): 27 | |
| Nutritional value: ● | |

P lace the peeled cloves of garlic in a saucepan with ½ litre/ 1 pint/ 2 cups of water and a pinch of salt; put on the lid and boil for 15 minutes. In the meantime toast the bread and sprinkle with the grated pecorino cheese. Take the saucepan off the heat, remove the garlic and mash it with a fork, then tip back into the boiling water along with a generous sprig of sage and a bay leaf. Season with salt and pepper. Arrange the toasted bread in the individual soup bowls, ladle over the *aïgo boulido* and trickle over a tablespoon of olive oil.

This simple, fragrant and wholesome soup can be savoured just as it is, or else heated briefly in the oven to dry out slightly, crisping the surface.

# BOUILLABAISSE

Fish soup ☞ *Provence*

**1** Clean and rinse all the fish and chop into pieces; split the lobster open lengthways. Clean the leek and the onion, chop them up finely and sauté lightly in a large casserole in 5-6 tablespoons of oil. Add the garlic and the tomato purée and allow the flavours to blend over a gentle heat.

**2** Tip in all the fish, season with salt and pepper, and add a couple of ladlefuls of hot water. Stir thoroughly. Add the saffron, a chopped sprig of parsley and a generous trickle of oil, and cook over a medium heat for half an hour. Toast the bread, and set a slice in each soup bowl, then ladle over the *bouillabaisse*.

800g/ 1 ¾ lb assorted soup fish (mullet, conger-eel or razor-clams, scorpion fish or gurnard, angler, redfish, mackerel, weever etc.)
4-5 red mullet
1 small lobster
200 g/ 7 oz sea bream or dog-fish
1 leek
1 spring onion
1-2 cloves garlic
300 g/ 11 oz tomato purée
Parsley
1-2 sachets of saffron powder
6 slices of bread
Olive oil
Salt and pepper

| | |
|---|---|
| Servings: 6 | |
| Preparation time: 30' | |
| Cooking time: 40' | |
| Difficulty: ● ● | |
| Flavour: ● | |
| Kcal (per serving): 597 | |
| Proteins (per serving): 45 | |
| Fats (per serving): 27 | |
| Nutritional value: ● | |

# CHAUDRÉE SAINTONGEAISE

La Rochelle fish soup ☛ *Saintonge and Aunis*

200 g/ 7 oz conger eel
200 g/ 7 oz ray
200 g/ 7 oz sole
200 g/ 7 oz cuttlefish
200 g/ 7 oz flounders
200 g/ 7 oz large shrimps
1/2 litre/ 1 pint/ 2 cups
   fish stock (made with cubes)
1/2 litre/ 1 pint/ 2 cups
   white wine
1 bouquet garni (parsley,
   bay leaves, thyme)
1 sprig tarragon
100 g/ 3 1/2 oz garlic
2 shallots
150 g/ 5 oz butter
100 g/ 3 1/2 oz baguette-type
   bread
Olive oil
Salt and pepper

| | |
|---|---|
| Servings: | 6 |
| Preparation time: | 20′ |
| Cooking time: | about 1 h |
| Difficulty: | ●●● |
| Flavour: | ●●● |
| Kcal (per serving): | 940 |
| Proteins (per serving): | 29 |
| Fats (per serving): | 72 |
| Nutritional value: | ●●● |

1 Melt 50 g/ 2 oz butter in an ovenproof earthenware casserole, then add the finely-chopped garlic, shallots and tarragon. Season with pepper, pour over the fish stock and the white wine, add the *bouquet garni* and cook for half an hour.

2 Meanwhile put two tablespoons of oil in a large frying-pan, add the cleaned and chopped fish, the cuttlefish and the shrimps and sauté gently.

3 Tip the fish into the casserole with the fish stock in the same order, cook for three minutes, then set in a pre-heated oven at 160°C for ten minutes. After this, remove the fish and keep warm, and pass the stock through a sieve.

**4** Pour the stock into a saucepan, add the remaining butter cut into flakes, and beat with a whisk, then season with salt and pepper. Slice the bread and rub the slices with garlic, then spread lightly with butter and toast briefly in the oven. Finally arrange the fish in a large, warmed soup tureen, pour over the stock and drop in the slices of bread.

# GARBURE

Vegetable soup ☞ *Béarn*

1 Bryonne pig's trotter
  (about 300 g/ 11 oz)
1 tender Savoy cabbage
300 g/ 11 oz shelled fresh
  white beans
500 g/ 1 lb 2 oz potatoes
3 carrots
2 leeks
2 cloves garlic
1 bunch thyme
Salt and pepper

Servings: 6-8
Preparation time: 30'+4-5 h
Cooking time: about 2 h
Difficulty: ● ●
Flavour: ● ● ●
Kcal (per serving): 386
Proteins (per serving): 26
Fats (per serving): 6
Nutritional value: ●

Steep the beans for 4-5 hours. Put the pig's trotter into a large saucepan with 3 litres/6 pints/12 cups of water and the bunch of thyme. Bring to the boil, then lower the heat and simmer for half an hour. Meanwhile trim the cabbage, discarding the stalk and the outer leaves, and slice. Drain the beans, peel the potatoes and cut into quarters; wash and trim the leeks and scrape the carrots, then chop both into fairly thick rings, and peel the garlic. Tip all the vegetables and the beans into the saucepan, season with salt and pepper and cook over a very gentle heat for an hour and a half.

# SOUPE AU PISTOU

Soup with basil and garlic sauce ☞ *Provence*

*"Pistou" is a sauce made from pounded garlic and basil blended with oil, very similar to the Ligurian "pesto", although without the pine kernels. In Provence it is widely used to enhance the flavour of soups and vegetable dishes.*

For the "pistou":
5-6 cloves garlic
150 g/ 5 oz basil leaves
4 ripe tomatoes (optional)
100 g/ 3 1/2 oz grated
  Parmesan cheese
Olive oil

For the soup:
1 onion
1 leek
2 ripe tomatoes
4 potatoes
200 g/ 7 oz French beans
  (haricots verts)
Vegetable stock
  (made with cube)
40 g/ 1 1/2 oz butter
Salt and pepper

| | |
|---|---|
| Servings: 4 | |
| Preparation time: 25'+15' | |
| Cooking time: 50' | |
| Difficulty: ● ● | |
| Flavour: ● ● ● | |
| Kcal (per serving): 447 | |
| Proteins (per serving): 12 | |
| Fats (per serving): 23 | |
| Nutritional value: ● ● | |

1 To make the *pistou*, wash, seed and peel the tomatoes (if you wish to include them). Remove the stems from the basil, and wash and dry the leaves. Whiz gently in the blender with the peeled cloves of garlic, the chopped tomatoes, and a pinch each of salt and pepper.

2 Tip the mixture into a bowl and gradually stir in the Parmesan cheese and 12-15 tablespoons of olive oil until the *pistou* thickens sufficiently; leave to rest for a few minutes.

Prepare the soup. Wash and trim the tomatoes and beans, and peel the potatoes. Peel the onion and leek and cut into thin slices, then sauté slowly in a casserole in the melted butter.
Add the chopped tomatoes, potatoes and beans, and season with salt and pepper to taste.
Pour over 1/2 litre/1 pint/ 2 cups of vegetable stock and leave to cook over a very gentle heat for about 45 minutes, adding extra stock from time to time if necessary.
Bring the soup to the table piping hot, serving the *pistou* separately so guests may help themselves. An extra trickle of olive oil will not go amiss.

# SOUPE À L'OIGNON

Onion Soup ☛ *Lyons region*

800 g/ 1 ³/₄ lb Spanish
  onions
150 g/ 5 oz Gruyère cheese
4 slices wholemeal bread
50 g/ 2 oz butter
1 level teaspoon sugar
1 litre/ 2 pints/ 4 cups
  good meat or chicken
  stock
Salt and pepper

| | |
|---|---|
| **Servings: 4** | |
| **Preparation time: 30′** | |
| **Cooking time: 1 h** | |
| **Difficulty:** ● ● | |
| **Flavour:** ● ● ● | |
| **Kcal (per serving): 520** | |
| **Proteins (per serving): 22** | |
| **Fats (per serving): 27** | |
| **Nutritional value:** ● ● ● | |

1 Switch on the oven at a low heat and dry out the slices of bread, without toasting them. Melt the butter in a large casserole then add the finely-sliced onions and season with salt and pepper. Cover the casserole and cook slowly for a quarter of an hour. Remove the lid, and continue cooking gently for 30 minutes, stirring the onions frequently with a wooden spoon.

2 Now add the sugar, and caramelise for 2 or 3 minutes.

3 Finally, pour over the stock, bring to the boil and simmer for a quarter of an hour.

At this point the soup is ready, but if you wish to serve it in the Lyons manner, that is au gratin, five minutes before serving pour into four ovenproof porcelain soup bowls, covering each with a slice of bread broken into two or three pieces which you should press lightly into the soup. Sprinkle with the grated cheese and toast in the oven for 5 minutes.

# SOUPE BOURGEOISE À LA SÉTOISE

Séte style fish soup ☛*Languedoc*

1 Clean the fish and molluscs and chop into pieces, eliminating all the bones. Slice the onion and sauté in two tablespoons of slightly warmed oil, then add the roughly-chopped tomatoes, the finely-chopped garlic and the white part of the leek, sliced.

2 Pour over the wine and the water, season with salt and generously with pepper, and sprinkle over a pinch of chilli powder. When it comes to the boil, tip in all the fish. Return to the boil, then lower the heat to minimum, cover, and cook for 40-45 minutes.

3 Bring a large saucepan of salted water to the boil a few minutes before the soup is ready, then tip in the vermicelli and drain while they are still *al dente*. Remove the fish pieces from the soup, and keep warm, then tip the vermicelli into the soup and cook for another 4-5 minutes. The fish should be served separately, with a little of the soup thickened either with flour or with two beaten eggs.

800 g/ 1 ¾ lb bass, sole, mullet, and redfish, sliced
8 crabs
4 prawns
3 ripe tomatoes
1 onion
1 clove garlic
1 leek

½ litre/ 1 pint/ 2 cups dry white wine
½ litre/ 1 pint/ 2 cups water
Powdered chilli pepper
250 g/ 9 oz vermicelli
Flour or 2 eggs
Olive oil
Salt and pepper

Servings: 6-8
Preparation time: 30'
Cooking time: 1 h 20'
Difficulty: ● ● ●
Flavour: ● ● ●
Kcal (per serving): 603
Proteins (per serving): 46
Fats (per serving): 11
Nutritional value: ● ● ●

# SOUPE DES VENDANGEURS

Harvest soup ☞ *Périgord*

500 g/1 lb 2 oz chicken giblets (liver, heart, gizzard)
1 leek
1 carrot
1 white turnip
1 stalk celery
1 onion spiked with a clove
1 clove garlic
1 bouquet garni
12 slices of stale wholemeal bread
200 g/ 7 oz Emmental cheese
50 g/ goose fat (or butter or lard)
Salt and pepper

| | |
|---|---|
| Servings: 6-8 | |
| Preparation time: 30' | |
| Cooking time: about 1h | |
| Difficulty: | ● ● |
| Flavour: | ● ● |
| Kcal (per serving): 847 | |
| Proteins (per serving): 40 | |
| Fats (per serving): 42 | |
| Nutritional value: | ● ● ● |

Wash and trim all the vegetables. Melt half the goose fat in a saucepan, then tip in the cleaned chicken giblets and brown over a lively heat for 5 minutes. Add the vegetables, the sliced garlic and onion and the *bouquet garni*, pour in 2 litres/ 4 pints/ 8 cups of water and season with salt and pepper. Bring to the boil, then skim the surface, lower the heat and cook for 45 minutes. In the meantime lightly fry the slices of bread in the rest of the goose fat, then arrange in a soup tureen in layers sprinkled with the grated cheese. Bring the stock back to the boil, sieve and pour over the bread in the soup tureen. Cover the tureen and leave to rest for 5 minutes before serving.

*Originally, in place of the chicken giblets, the principal ingredient of this recipe was the goose carcass left over from the preparation of the confit.*

*A manor in the historic region of Périgord.*

# SOUPE DE MOULES COMME AU GRAU-DU-ROI

## Cream of mussel soup  Languedoc

Put the sliced onions, the garlic, rosemary, thyme, bay leaf, wine and water into a large saucepan. Bring to the boil, then lower the heat and simmer for a quarter of an hour. Sieve the stock and then pour half of it, with the same quantity of water, into another saucepan; tip in the thoroughly-cleaned mussels and cook them until they open.

Put the rest of the sieved stock into a casserole and add the mussels after removing the shells, keeping a few whole aside to garnish the dish. Sieve the stock in which you cooked the mussels into a saucepan, then put the food-mill over it and pass through the mussels along with the stock. Reheat the resulting fish purée, stirring thoroughly over a gentle heat. Finally stir in the juice of the lemon and the cream, seasoning with salt and pepper if necessary.

2 onions
3-4 sprigs thyme
1 bay leaf
1 sprig rosemary
3 cloves garlic
1 bottle dry white wine
$1/2$ litre/ 1 pint/ 2 cups water
2 kg/ 4 $1/2$ lb mussels
1 lemon
50 g/ 2 oz double or cooking cream
Salt and pepper

| | |
|---|---|
| Servings: | 6 |
| Preparation time: | 20' |
| Cooking time: | about 30' |
| Difficulty: | ● ● |
| Flavour: | ● ● ● |
| Kcal (per serving): | 305 |
| Proteins (per serving): | 21 |
| Fats (per serving): | 8 |
| Nutritional value: | ● ● ● |

500 g/ 1 lb 2 oz conger
 eel (with head)
2 gurnard
the head of a sea bream
500 g/ 1 lb 2 oz angler
1 kg/ 2 1/4 lb mussels
10 prawns
2 onions
2 cloves garlic
1/2 litre/1 pint/ 2 cups rosé wine
1 bouquet garni (tarragon,
 thyme, bay leaf)
1 small red pepper
1 dried chilli pepper
2 large, ripe tomatoes
1 stalk celery
Flour
Parsley
Slices of bread rubbed with garlic
Olive oil
Salt and pepper

| | |
|---|---|
| **Servings:** 4 | |
| **Preparation time:** 40' | |
| **Cooking time:** 1 h 15' | |
| **Difficulty:** ● ● ● | |
| **Flavour:** ● ● | |
| **Kcal (per serving):** 377 | |
| **Proteins (per serving):** 51 | |
| **Fats (per serving):** 13 | |
| **Nutritional value:** ● ● | |

# Ttoro

Fish soup ☛ *Pays Basque*

Break all the fish heads, including those of the gurnard, into at least two pieces, tip into a large saucepan and sweat in two tablespoons of oil. Add the chopped onion and garlic and sauté until lightly-coloured, then pour over the wine, 1½ litres/ 3 pints/ 6 cups of water, and add the *bouquet garni*. Clean the pepper, removing the seeds and the white membranes, then cut into thin strips, crush the chilli pepper, peel and roughly chop the tomatoes and the celery, then tip all into the saucepan with the fish heads and season with salt. Cover the saucepan and cook gently for an hour. Chop all the fish flesh into pieces, coat lightly in flour and fry for a minute each side in a frying-pan in two tablespoons of oil. Sprinkle with salt, and leave to drain on kitchen paper. After an hour sieve the fish stock, pressing it thoroughly through the sieve to extract all the juices. Clean the mussels, then arrange the fish pieces in a large casserole, scatter over the mussels and pour over the stock. Bring to the boil and cook slowly for 5 minutes. Finally add the prawns and cook a further 5 minutes. Sprinkle with chopped parsley and serve the fish soup piping hot, spooning it over slices of lightly toasted bread rubbed with garlic.

# LES VIANDES

*Farms and woodland, meadows and pastures:
all the flavours of tradition in these superb dishes
which are as much a feast for the eyes as for the palate.*

3

# ÉPAULE D'AGNEAU AU CHOU

Lamb rolls wrapped in cabbage ☞ *Normandy*

1 boned shoulder of lamb
  1.2-1.4 kg/ 2 1/2 -3 lb
1 bunch basil
Pig's omentum (suet jackets)
1 bouquet garni
6 leaves of Savoy cabbage
1/2 litre/ 1 pint/ 2 cups
  good stock
Olive oil
Salt and pepper

*For the sauce:*
3 shallots
1/4 litre/ 1/2 pint/ 1 cup
  red wine
A knob of butter

*For the roux:*
3 tablespoons flour
3 tablespoons butter
Salt and pepper

| | |
|---|---|
| Servings: 6 | |
| Preparation time: 40'+48 h | |
| Cooking time: 2 h 45' | |
| Difficulty: ● ● ● | |
| Flavour: ● ● ● | |
| Kcal (per serving): 867 | |
| Proteins (per serving): 44 | |
| Fats (per serving): 64 | |
| Nutritional value: ● ● ● | |

1 Divide the shoulder into six equal pieces and set them to marinate in half a glass of oil with the basil, salt and pepper. It's no surprise to find oil and basil in Normandy, since all traditions adapt to remain vital. Leave in a cool place for 48 hours, turning frequently. Blanch the cabbage leaves for 3 minutes in salted water, then dry them and place a piece of lamb on each leaf, roll up and wrap in a small section of pig's omentum. Lay the six bundles in an ovenproof dish, add the *bouquet garni* and pour over the stock. Cover with a sheet of aluminium foil and cook in a preheated oven at 150°C for two and a half hours.
While the lamb is cooking, trim and chop the shallots. Sauté lightly in the melted butter, then pour over the red wine and season with salt and pepper. Continue cooking until the sauce is reduced to half its volume, then sieve and set aside.

2 Remove the lamb from the oven, then arrange the rolls close to each other in a casserole. Now prepare the *roux*, gently melting the butter and blending in the flour smoothly over a low heat, without letting it colour. Gradually pour in the wine sauce, stirring delicately all the time, and enough of the lamb cooking juices to produce a smooth, creamy sauce. Adjust salt and pepper to taste, then pour over the lamb rolls. Set the casserole over the lowest possible heat, and cook for a further 15 minutes.

# GIGOT D'AGNEAU À LA BRETONNE

Leg of lamb with beans ☛ *Brittany*

1 Set the beans to steep. The length of time required for steeping depends on the age of the beans, that is how long they have been dried; if over a year has passed, then they will need to steep for 24 hours, but normally 4-5 hours are sufficient. After this, drain, and tip them into a large saucepan with the onion spiked with the clove, the scraped and roughly chopped carrots, the *bouquet garni* and the crushed peppercorns. Cover with cold water and bring slowly to the boil, then put the lid on the saucepan and cook over a very gentle heat for about an hour and a quarter.

In the meantime make slits in the leg of lamb and stuff them with thin slices of peeled garlic. Set the meat in a well-buttered roasting-tin, season with salt and pepper and cook for 30 minutes at 200°C, then lower the temperature to 180°C and continue cooking for an hour, basting every so often with the bean cooking water.

After this, remove the lamb and switch off the oven. Wrap the roast leg in aluminium foil, set it on a dish and keep warm on the lowered door of the oven.

2 Sauté the sliced onions lightly in the rest of the butter, add the peeled, seeded and diced tomatoes and stir into the drained beans. Season with salt and pepper.

Arrange the beans on a large serving dish, lay the slices of lamb over them and spoon over the cooking juices.

---

1 leg of saltmarsh
  lamb (gigot)
  of 1.5 kg/ 3 ½ lb
500 g dried white beans
1 onion spiked with a clove
1 bay leaf
3 carrots
1 bouquet garni
  (parsley, thyme,
  bay leaf)
10 whole peppercorns
2 cloves garlic
100 g/ 3 ½ oz butter
2 onions
2 tomatoes
Salt and pepper

| | |
|---|---|
| **Servings: 4** | |
| **Preparation time: 20'+4-5 h** | |
| **Cooking time: 3 h** | |
| **Difficulty:** | ● ● |
| **Flavour:** | ● ● ● |
| **Kcal (per serving): 637** | |
| **Proteins (per serving): 58** | |
| **Fats (per serving): 21** | |
| **Nutritional value:** | ● ● |

# PARMENTIER D'AGNEAU

Lamb and potato gratin ☛ *Burgundy and Champagne*

1 kg/ 2 ¼ lb boned saddle
  of lamb
500 g/ 1 lb 2 oz potatoes
125 g/ 4 oz Époisses cheese
  (typical strong-flavoured
  Burgundy cows' cheese)
15 tablespoons milk
20 g/ ²/₃ oz butter
2 cloves garlic
Olive oil
Salt and pepper

| | |
|---|---|
| Servings: 4-6 | |
| Preparation time: 1 h | |
| Cooking time: 35' | |
| Difficulty: ● ● ● | |
| Flavour: ● ● ● | |
| Kcal (per serving): 582 | |
| Proteins (per serving): 62 | |
| Fats (per serving): 25 | |
| Nutritional value: ● ● | |

1 Cut four fillets from the saddle of lamb and set them aside. Chop the remainder, season with salt and pepper and sauté in a frying-pan in a tablespoon of oil; leave to cool then mince.

2 Prepare the potato purée. Boil the potatoes, then peel them and mash thoroughly. Stir in the milk and the butter and finally the cheese chopped into pieces, blending it in until it is completely melted, and season with salt and pepper.

3 Butter an ovenproof dish and arrange half the purée in the bottom; lay the minced lamb over this then cover with the rest of the purée.

Salt and pepper the fillets of lamb and cook for 7-8 minutes in a tablespoon of oil, then remove from the heat, lay on a warm plate and cover with a sheet of aluminium foil.
Pour the fat out of the frying-pan, tip in ¼ litre/ ½ pint/ 1 cup of water, and the peeled and crushed garlic cloves. Bring to the boil, scraping the bottom of the pan with a spoon; continue cooking until the liquid has reduced to a couple of spoonfuls, then sieve. Brown the gratin for 4-5 minutes under the grill; slice the fillets thinly, spoon over the garlic sauce and serve with the lamb and potato gratin.

*The Joly bridge in Semur spans the river Armançon, one of the tributaries of the Yonne.*

# BŒUF À LA MODE

Braised beef and veal ☛ *Île-de-France*

**1** Start the day before. Salt and pepper the beef and set it in a bowl with one sliced carrot, one thinly sliced onion, the *bouquet garni*, the white wine and the brandy. Cover and leave to marinate in a cool place. The next day, remove from the marinade, drain and dry thoroughly, then sieve the marinade, keeping the *bouquet garni* aside.

**2** Heat the butter in a large, preferably cast-iron, casserole, then brown the meat on all sides; remove it briefly from the casserole and dilute the cooking residue. Replace the meat in the casserole along with the marinade, and cook until the liquid is reduced by half. Tip in the calf's foot, the remaining carrots and onions, the shallots and the garlic all finely chopped. Replace the *bouquet garni*, season with salt and pepper and pour over the stock. Bring to the boil, skim the surface and then lower the heat, cover the casserole and cook for three hours.

1.5 kg/ 3 1/2 lb lean beef, wrapped in fatty bacon and tied up like a roast
3 carrots
3 onions
2 shallots
1 clove garlic
30 g/ 1 oz butter
1 bouquet garni
1 boned calf's foot
1/4 litre/ 1/2 pint/ 1 cup meat stock
1/4 litre/ 1/2 pint/ 1 cup dry white wine
4 tablespoons brandy
Salt and pepper

| | |
|---|---|
| Servings: 6 | |
| Preparation time: 30' | |
| Cooking time: 3 h | |
| Difficulty: ● ● | |
| Flavour: ● ● ● | |
| Kcal (per serving): 943 | |
| Proteins (per serving): 46 | |
| Fats (per serving): 57 | |
| Nutritional value: ● ● ● | |

# Bœuf Bourguignon

Beef Burgundy style ☞ *Burgundy*

1.5 kg/ 3 1/2 lb
  stewing beef
50 g/ 2 oz butter
100 g/ 3 1/2 oz
  fresh bacon
2 carrots
2 onions
30 g/ 1 oz flour
2 cloves garlic
1 1/2 bottles red Burgundy
1 bouquet garni (parsley, leek,
  thyme and bay leaves)
Olive oil
Salt and pepper

| | |
|---|---|
| **Servings:** | 4-6 |
| **Preparation time:** | 20' |
| **Cooking time:** | about 3 h |
| **Difficulty:** | ● ● |
| **Flavour:** | ● ● ● |
| **Kcal (per serving):** | 716 |
| **Proteins (per serving):** | 43 |
| **Fats (per serving):** | 44 |
| **Nutritional value:** | ● ● |

**1** In a casserole brown the diced bacon, the chopped beef, and the sliced carrots and onions in the butter and 5 tablespoons of oil.

**2** Sprinkle over the flour and stir in to coat all the ingredients, then pour over the wine, add the crushed garlic and the *bouquet garni*, and season with salt and pepper.
Cover and cook over very low heat for 2 1/2 hours. Remove the meat and the vegetables from the casserole and reduce the sauce if it is too liquid. Replace the meat in the casserole, adjust salt to taste, and serve.

# CARBONNADE

Beef stewed in beer ☞ *Flanders*

1.5 kg/3 ½ lb stewing beef,
  in chunks
100 g/ 3 ½ oz lard
3 tablespoons flour
3 tablespoons vinegar
3 tablespoons
  brown sugar
1 litre/ 2 pints/ 4 cups beer
4 slices spice bread
300 g/ 11 oz onions
1 sprig thyme
1 bay leaf
2 cloves
Salt and pepper

| | |
|---|---|
| Servings: 6 | |
| Preparation time: 40' | |
| Cooking time: 3 h | |
| Difficulty: ● ● | |
| Flavour: ● ● ● | |
| Kcal (per serving): 598 | |
| Proteins (per serving): 49 | |
| Fats (per serving): 20 | |
| Nutritional value: ● ● ● | |

Sprinkle the chunks of beef with salt and pepper, then melt the lard in a large casserole and brown the beef for 4 minutes. Sprinkle in the flour and mix it in well, then add the chopped onions and cook for 5 minutes.
Dilute the cooking residue with the vinegar, then pour over the beer and ½ litre/ 1 pint/ 2 cups water. Stir in the sugar, the thyme, the bay leaf and the cloves, and cover with the slices of spice bread. Season with salt and pepper, put the lid on the casserole and cook very slowly for three hours, adding more beer or water if necessary.

# BŒUF EN DAUBE

Beef casserole *Provence*

| | |
|---|---|
| 800 g/1 ¾ lb stewing beef | |
| 80 g/ 3 oz fatty bacon | |
| 200 g/ 7 oz tomato purée | |
| 2 onions | |
| 1 carrot | |
| 4 cloves garlic | |
| 1 bouquet garni (sage, parsley, bay leaf, thyme, rosemary) | |
| Orange peel | |
| Cloves | |
| Red wine | |
| Olive oil | |
| Salt and whole peppercorns | |

| | |
|---|---|
| **Servings: 4** | |
| **Preparation time: 15′** | |
| **Cooking time: 2 h 40′** | |
| **Difficulty:** ● ● | |
| **Flavour:** ● ● | |
| **Kcal (per serving): 491** | |
| **Proteins (per serving): 43** | |
| **Fats (per serving): 25** | |
| **Nutritional value:** ● ● | |

1 Peel the onions, spiking one with 3 or 4 cloves, then cut into wedges. Scrape and slice the carrot, then wash and trim the herbs and tie up the *bouquet garni*.

2 Cut the bacon into strips and sauté in a large casserole in 4 tablespoons of oil, along with the onions and the carrot. Add the tomato purée, the garlic, the *bouquet garni*, a little grated orange peel, a pinch of salt and a few peppercorns. After 5-6 minutes add the chunks of beef and cover with red wine. Put the lid on the casserole and bring rapidly to the boil, then lower the heat and cook very slowly for at least two and a half hours, keeping the lid on. Add more wine, if and when necessary, and adjust salt and pepper to taste.

43

# FRICANDEAU

## Larded veal ☞*Alsace*

800 g/ 1 ¾ lb rump veal in a single slice, 4 cm/ 2 in high
100 g/ 3 ½ oz fatty bacon
2 carrots
2 onions
1 tablespoon tomato concentrate
½ litre/ 1 pint/ 2 cups dry white wine
⅓ litre/ ⅔ pint/1 ⅓ cups meat stock
35 g/ 1 ⅓ oz butter
Olive oil
Salt and pepper

| | |
|---|---|
| Servings: 4 | |
| Preparation time: 30′ | |
| Cooking time: 2 h 30′ | |
| Difficulty: ● ● | |
| Flavour: ● ● ● | |
| Kcal (per serving): 560 | |
| Proteins (per serving): 45 | |
| Fats (per serving): 18 | |
| Nutritional value: ● ● | |

Make slits in the veal and insert the bacon cut into thin strips, then tie it up if necessary to keep its shape. Heat 15 g/ ½ oz of butter and two tablespoons of oil in a large frying-pan, and brown the meat for 2 minutes on each side. Remove from the heat. Scrape and slice the carrots and peel and finely slice the onions. Melt the remaining butter in an ovenproof dish, and sweat the vegetables in it, then lay the meat on top. Pour over the wine, season with salt and pepper, cover and bring to the boil, then transfer immediately to the oven, pre-heated to 180°C. After an hour, remove the dish from the oven and replace on the hotplate. Pour over the stock, in which you have diluted the tomato concentrate, then bring to the boil again and replace in the oven for another hour. After this, remove the veal and the vegetables and place them on an ovenproof serving dish. Reduce the cooking juices until they are thick and syrupy, then pour over the meat and replace in the oven for 5 minutes before serving.

*A view of the Alsace countryside.*

# GARDIANNE

Aromatic stew *Languedoc*

1.5 kg/ 3 1/2 lb bull's meat
  or mature beef
100 g/ 3 1/2 oz bacon
2 onions
2 tablespoons flour
Olive oil

*For the marinade*:
1 1/2 bottles red wine
3 onions
3 cloves garlic, crushed
2 carrots
1 celery stalk
2 bay leaves
2 sprigs thyme
2 cloves
The peel of 1 orange
Salt and whole
  peppercorns

| | |
|---|---|
| **Servings: 6** | |
| **Preparation time: 20'+24 h** | |
| **Cooking time: about 2 h** | |
| **Difficulty:** ● ● | |
| **Flavour:** ● ● ● | |
| **Kcal (per serving): 579** | |
| **Proteins (per serving): 47** | |
| **Fats (per serving): 18** | |
| **Nutritional value:** ● ● | |

1 Chop the meat into fairly large chunks and put them into a large bowl with all the marinade ingredients. Season with salt and add a tablespoon of whole peppercorns. Cover and leave to marinate in a cool place for 24 hours. The next day, remove the chunks of meat, squeeze them out thoroughly and lay on a plate. Sieve the marinade, pour it into a casserole and heat without letting it boil.

2 In another large casserole brown the two thinly-sliced onions in 4-5 tablespoons of oil; add the meat and sprinkle over the flour. Brown the chunks of meat all over, then pour in the hot marinade. Cover and cook for a generous two hours over a very gentle heat. If the sauce is still too liquid, remove the lid and raise the heat until it reduces sufficiently. The *gardianne* is normally served with either boiled rice or steamed potatoes.

# DAUBE DE VEAU

Braised veal ☛ *Les Landes*

1.5 kg/ 3 ½ lb rump veal
150 g/ 5 oz prugnoli,
   cantarelli or cultivated
   mushrooms
4 onions
2 carrots
2 tablespoons lard
10 tablespoons
   tomato purée
½ litre/ 1 pint/ 2 cups
   meat stock
Nutmeg
2 cloves
1 stalk celery
1 thick slice raw ham
Salt and pepper

| | |
|---|---|
| Servings: 4-6 | |
| Preparation time: 20′ | |
| Cooking time: 2 h 40′ | |
| Difficulty: | ● ● |
| Flavour: | ● ● |
| Kcal (per serving): 540 | |
| Proteins (per serving): 45 | |
| Fats (per serving): 14 | |
| Nutritional value: | ● ● |

1 Heat the lard in a large saucepan and brown the meat on all sides, then transfer it to a large casserole (one with a lid).

2 Peel the onions and slice finely, then scrape and slice the carrots. Tip both into the saucepan with the lard and sauté lightly, then add the tomato purée. Cook for 3-4 minutes, then pour the sauce over the veal in the casserole.

3 Replace the saucepan on the heat, pour in the stock and bring to the boil. Pour the stock too over the veal, then season with salt and pepper and add a teaspoon of grated nutmeg, the cloves and the roughly-chopped celery. Put the lid on the casserole and cook over a very gentle heat for 2 hours.

4 Clean the mushrooms and dice the ham. Tip both into the meat casserole after the 2 hours are up. Mix thoroughly and continue cooking for about 40 minutes, then serve.

# HACHUA

Veal with chilli peppers 🖛 *Pays Basque*

1.3 kg/ 3 lb loin of veal
4 tablespoons goose fat
  or lard
4 onions
4 cloves garlic
10 fresh green chilli peppers
Powdered chilli pepper
Salt and pepper

| | |
|---|---|
| Servings: 4-6 | |
| Preparation time: 20' | |
| Cooking time: 1 h 15' | |
| Difficulty: ● ● | |
| Flavour: ● ● ● | |
| Kcal (per serving): 383 | |
| Proteins (per serving): 51 | |
| Fats (per serving): 17 | |
| Nutritional value: ● ● | |

Heat half the goose fat in a casserole and sauté very lightly the thinly-sliced onions and the cleaned and sliced green chillies, then remove from the casserole and set aside. Chop the veal into ¹/₂ cm/ ¹/₄ in cubes, then brown in the remaining goose fat in the casserole. Stir well, season with salt, then add half a teaspoon of powdered chilli pepper and the cloves of garlic, peeled and sliced and with the green germ removed. Cook slowly for about ten minutes, then add the onions and chillies. Season with salt, cover the casserole and cook gently for an hour.

# CAILLES DE STANISLAS

Stanislas quail ☛*Lorraine*

8 quail, with backbone
  removed
1 chicken breast
4 tablespoons single cream
80 g/ 3 oz foie gras
80 g/ 3 oz butter
White wine
1 shallot
80 g/ 3 oz black truffle
Olive oil
Salt and pepper

| | |
|---|---|
| Servings: 4 | |
| Preparation time: 25' | |
| Cooking time: 45' | |
| Difficulty: ● ● | |
| Flavour: ● ● | |
| Kcal (per serving): 593 | |
| Proteins (per serving): 36 | |
| Fats (per serving): 40 | |
| Nutritional value: ● ● ● | |

Dice the chicken breast and tip it into the blender with the cream and half the black truffle sliced, seasoning with salt and pepper. Divide the *foie gras* into eight pieces and use it and the chicken and truffle mixture to stuff the quail. Sew up the aperture securely and arrange the quail in a roasting-tin greased with 30 g/ 1 oz of butter, dribbling a trickle of oil over them. Arrange the backbones (which you should make sure the butcher gives you) in between the quail, and sprinkle over the chopped shallot. Cook in a pre-heated oven at 220°C for half an hour, basting the quail with their cooking juices half-way through. When cooked, keep the quail warm and dilute the roasting-tin cooking juices with half a glass of wine. Reduce and filter the sauce then add the remaining butter, beating well with an egg-whisk, and the rest of the truffle. Place two quail on each plate, pour over the sauce, and serve.

*The gate in the city walls in Verdun, on the banks of the Meuse.*

# BLANCS DE CANARD AU MIEL

Duck breast in honey ☞ *Burgundy*

2 duck breasts (350 g/12 oz each)
2 cooking apples
400 ml/ 3/4 pint/ 1 1/2 cups
   cider
200 ml/ 6 fl oz/ 3/4 cup
   chicken stock
50 g/ 2 oz butter
2 teaspoons honey
Salt and pepper

| | |
|---|---|
| Servings: 4 | |
| Preparation time: 20' | |
| Cooking time: 30' | |
| Difficulty: ● ● | |
| Flavour: ● | |
| Kcal (per serving): 302 | |
| Proteins (per serving): 28 | |
| Fats (per serving): 15 | |
| Nutritional value: ● ● | |

1 Heat a frying-pan thoroughly and cook the duck breasts without adding any extra fat. Season with salt and pepper, cooking for 10 minutes on the skin side and 5 on the other, then remove from the pan and keep warm.

2 Rinse the apples and slice them without peeling, then tip them into the frying-pan and cook for 10 minutes, stirring all the time, until nicely-coloured.

3 Pour the fat out of the frying-pan and replace it with the cider mixed with the chicken stock and seasoned with salt and pepper. Add the honey and the butter cut into flakes, beating well with an egg-whisk. Finally, slice the duck breasts not too finely, and arrange the slices on the heated individual plates along with the apples; pour the sauce over and serve immediately.

*Nevers, on the banks of the Loire.*

# Canard nantais rôti dans son jus au Muscadet

Duck in Muscadet ☞ *Nantes region*

1 duck of about 2.5 kg/ 6 lb
1/2 bottle dry white wine
   (Muscadet)
1 onion
1 carrot
1 clove garlic
100 g/ 3 1/2 oz butter
Olive oil
Salt and pepper

| | |
|---|---|
| Servings: 6-8 | |
| Preparation time: 20′ | |
| Cooking time: 1 h 40′ | |
| Difficulty: ● ● | |
| Flavour: ● ● ● | |
| Kcal (per serving): 721 | |
| Proteins (per serving): 57 | |
| Fats (per serving): 30 | |
| Nutritional value: ● ● ● | |

*A detail of the Ducal Castle in Nantes.*

Rub the duck thoroughly with salt and pepper inside and out. Heat up a sufficiently large roasting-tin on the hot plate, and put in the neck and the wings cut into pieces. Anoint the duck with a tablespoon of oil and a knob of butter, then set it into the tin resting on one side and put into the oven, pre-heated to 250°C. After 25 minutes turn the bird over onto the other side and cook for a further 25 minutes. After this rest the duck on its back and cook for another 45 minutes, basting it frequently with the cooking juices, then remove from the oven and keep warm.

Throw away almost all the cooking fat, then tip in the chopped carrot and onion and the finely-chopped garlic. As soon as these begin to colour, pour over the wine and a glass of water, reduce the liquid by a quarter and adjust salt to taste. In a small saucepan cook the butter until it turns hazel-coloured (*beurre noisette*) then stir it into the sieved wine sauce. Serve separately.

# GÂTEAU DE FOIES DE VOLAILLE

Liver tart ☞ *Lyons region*

**1** Trim and clean the chicken livers, then season with salt and pepper. Tip them into a bowl, pour over the wine and leave to marinate in a cool place for a couple of hours. Drain, then whiz in the blender and tip the resulting purée into a large bowl.

**2** Stir the whole eggs, the cream, the melted butter and the cognac into the liver mixture and blend in until you have a smooth creamy paste. Season with salt and pepper and add a tablespoon of chopped parsley. Butter an ovenproof porcelain mould, pour in the liver paste and set the mould in a cold water bain-marie. Cook in a pre-heated oven at 180°C for 45 minutes. The "tart" can then be served with your preferred sauce: Nantua, Madeira or Financier, all of which can generally be found ready-made in good delicatessen shops.

15-16 chicken livers
5 eggs
150 g/ 5 oz butter
130 g/ 4 1/2 oz double or cooking cream
2 glasses dry white wine
1 measure cognac
Chopped parsley
Salt and pepper

| | |
|---|---|
| Servings: 6 | |
| Preparation time: 30' | |
| Cooking time: 45' | |
| Difficulty: ● ● | |
| Flavour: ● ● | |
| Kcal (per serving): 882 | |
| Proteins (per serving): 18 | |
| Fats (per serving): 40 | |
| Nutritional value: ● ● ● | |

# BARDATTE

Cabbage stuffed with rabbit 🖝 *Brittany*

1 Savoy cabbage
2 onions
50 g/ 2 oz butter
500 g/ 1 lb 2oz rabbit meat
2 slices bread
100 g/ 3 $^1/_2$ oz cultivated
    mushrooms
1 glass milk
1 egg
1 tablespoon fresh thyme leaves
1 broad thin sheet of bacon
    fat to wrap up the cabbage
$^1/_3$ litre/ $^2/_3$ pint/ 1 $^1/_2$ cups
    Muscadet or other
    dry white wine
$^1/_3$ litre/ $^2/_3$ pint/ 1 $^1/_2$ cups
    chicken stock
Salt and pepper

| | |
|---|---|
| Servings: 4-6 | |
| Preparation time: 30' | |
| Cooking time: 2h 30' | |
| Difficulty: ●●● | |
| Flavour: ●● | |
| Kcal (per serving): 833 | |
| Proteins (per serving): 41 | |
| Fats (per serving): 31 | |
| Nutritional value: ●●● | |

1 Discard the tougher outside leaves of the cabbage and the stalk, then blanch it for 10 minutes in salted water. Drain and keep to one side.

*A view of Dinan, in Brittany.*

2 Slice the onions and the mushrooms, then sauté for 10 minutes in the melted butter in a casserole. Remove from the heat, add the chopped rabbit meat, the bread soaked in the milk and then squeezed, the egg and the thyme. Mix well, and season with salt and pepper.

**3** Open out the leaves of the cabbage and remove the heart. Arrange the stuffing between the leaves, with at least a third in the central cavity of the cabbage.

**4** Close up the cabbage again as best you can, then wrap it up in the sheet of bacon fat and secure well. Finally place in a fairly deep ovenproof dish, and pour over the wine and the stock. Cover the dish with a double layer of aluminium foil, then set in the oven at 180°C and cook for 2 hours. Every so often, lift the foil and baste the cabbage with its cooking juices.

# LAPIN PROVENÇAL

Provençal rabbit ☞ *Provence*

1 rabbit, 1.3 kg/ 3 lb
3 ripe tomatoes, 2 cloves garlic
Mustard
Flour
Vegetable stock
  (made with cube)
Dry white wine
Olive oil
Salt, pepper and whole black
  peppercorns

| | |
|---|---|
| Servings: 4 | |
| Preparation time: 25'+2 h | |
| Cooking time: 50' | |
| Difficulty: | ● ● |
| Flavour: | ● ● |
| Kcal (per serving): 468 | |
| Proteins (per serving): 46 | |
| Fats (per serving): 18 | |
| Nutritional value: | ● ● |

Wash and dry the rabbit and cut it into 10-12 pieces. Brown these in a saucepan in 4 tablespoons of oil, seasoning lightly with salt. Remove the rabbit and pour off the oil, then tip in a glass of stock and warm it over a moderate heat. Coat the rabbit pieces lightly in flour, then replace in the saucepan. Let the flavours blend, then pour over a glass of wine, and adjust salt and pepper to taste. Clean, peel and seed the tomatoes; chop them roughly, then add to the meat along with the garlic, 3 or 4 peppercorns and a teaspoon of mustard. Cook over a very gentle heat, adding more stock a little at a time as required. When the rabbit is cooked (about 50 minutes altogether), arrange the pieces on a serving-dish, then pour over the sieved sauce. Serve with boiled French beans and salad.

# PIGEONS EN MARINADE

Marinated pigeons ☞ *Burgundy and Champagne*

4 pigeons of about 400 g/ 14 oz
  each
50 g/ 2 oz onions
50 g/ 2 oz carrots
20 g/ $^2$/$_3$ butter
400 ml/ $^3$/$_4$ pint/ 1 $^1$/$_2$ cups
  single cream
$^1$/$_2$ litre/ 1 pint/ 2 cups red wine
5 tablespoons vinegar
5 tablespoons Marc de Bourgogne
  (brandy)
1 clove garlic, 1 bouquet garni
Salt and pepper

| | |
|---|---|
| **Servings: 4** | |
| **Preparation time: 20'+5-6 h** | |
| **Cooking time: 40'** | |
| **Difficulty:** | ● ● |
| **Flavour:** | ● ● ● |
| **Kcal (per serving): 672** | |
| **Proteins (per serving): 42** | |
| **Fats (per serving): 26** | |
| **Nutritional value:** | ● ● |

1 Put the four pigeons into a large bowl with the chopped onions, the sliced carrots and the crushed clove of garlic; pour over the wine and the vinegar and add the *bouquet garni*. Cover and put in the fridge for 5-6 hours. Remove the pigeons from the marinade, dry them, then rub with salt and pepper inside and out. In an ovenproof casserole, brown them in 20 g/$^2$/$_3$ oz of butter, then set in a pre-heated oven at 200°C and cook for 20-25 minutes.

2 Remove from the oven, take the pigeons out of the casserole and keep warm, then dilute the cooking residue in the casserole with the brandy over a very gentle heat. Pour in the marinade liquid and reduce to half over a rapid heat.
Add the cream, and leave to reduce further until you have a smooth, creamy sauce. Season with salt and pepper, then sieve and pour over the quartered pigeons.

# PINTADE AU CHOU

Guinea-fowl with cabbage *Lyons region*

| |
|---|
| 1 guinea-fowl, tied up and ready to cook |
| 1 small Savoy cabbage |
| 200 g / 7 oz smoked bacon |
| 50 g / 2 oz butter |
| Salt and pepper |

| | |
|---|---|
| **Servings:** | 4-6 |
| **Preparation time:** | 30' |
| **Cooking time:** | 1 h 50' |
| **Difficulty:** | ● ● ● |
| **Flavour:** | ● ● |
| **Kcal (per serving):** | 814 |
| **Proteins (per serving):** | 64 |
| **Fats (per serving):** | 55 |
| **Nutritional value:** | ● ● ● |

1 Divide the cabbage into four and throw away the outer leaves, the tougher ribs and the stalk. Blanch for 5 minutes and drain well. Put the diced bacon into a large casserole and sauté until cooked, stirring all the time, then remove and put in the cabbage.

2 Cook slowly for 10 minutes, then season with salt and pepper. Tip the bacon back in with the cabbage, cover and cook for a quarter of an hour. At the same time, grease the guinea-fowl with half the melted butter, sprinkle with salt and cook in a pre-heated oven at 240-250 ° for 15 minutes.

3 When it is nicely browned, remove the guinea-fowl and set it in the middle of the cabbage in the casserole, pressing it down well. Cover and cook slowly for 1 hour 20 minutes.

4 Arrange the cabbage in a deep serving dish, laying the pieces of guinea-fowl on top, then sprinkle over the diced bacon. Having left the casserole on the heat, reduce the cooking juices, then beat in the rest of the butter with an egg-whisk; serve the sauce separately.

# BÄCKEOFFE

## Mixed meat casserole ☛Alsace

500 g/ 1 lb 2 oz boned pork
   shoulder
500 g/ 1 lb 2 oz boned
   shoulder of mutton
500 g/ 1 lb 2 oz beef brisket
1 kg/ 2 1/4 lb potatoes
1 kg/ 2 1/4 lb onions
2 cloves garlic
1/2 litre dry
   white Alsace wine
1 bouquet garni
1 tablespoon of chopped
   parsley
2 sprigs thyme
1 bay leaf
2 tablespoons lard
Salt and pepper

| | |
|---|---|
| Servings: 8 | |
| Preparation time: 30'+24 h | |
| Cooking time: about 4 hours | |
| Difficulty: ● ● | |
| Flavour: ● ● ● | |
| Kcal (per serving): 1587 | |
| Proteins (per serving): 60 | |
| Fats (per serving): 101 | |
| Nutritional value: ● ● ● | |

1 Chop all the meat into chunks as for stew and set to marinate for 24 hours in a large bowl with the wine, 2 onions, the crushed garlic, the *bouquet garni*, salt and pepper. The next day, peel the potatoes and the remaining onions and slice them not too thin. Then take a large earthenware casserole with lid and grease it well with lard. Arrange a layer of potatoes in the bottom, followed by a layer of meat and then one of onions.

2 Season with salt and pepper, sprinkle with the herbs, then build up further layers of potatoes, meat and onions, ending with a layer of potatoes. Season again with salt and pepper. Discarding the *bouquet garni* and the onions, pour the wine from the marinade into the casserole until it reaches the top layer. If there is not enough liquid, supplement with water or stock. Cover the casserole (preferably sealing around the lid with a strip of paste made from flour and water) then cook in a preheated oven at 160°C for 4 hours.

# CAQHUSE

Baked pork with onions ☞*Picardy*

1.2 kg/ 2 ¹/₂ lb pork,
   in one slice 3-4 cm/1 ¹/₂
   in high, cut from the ham
600 g/ 1 ¹/₄ lb onions
100 g/ 3 ¹/₂ oz butter
30 g/ 1 oz lard
3 tablespoons cider
   vinegar
Salt and pepper

| | |
|---|---|
| Servings: 6 | |
| Preparation time: 20' | |
| Cooking time: 1 h 30' | |
| Difficulty: ● ● | |
| Flavour: ● ● | |
| Kcal (per serving): 531 | |
| Proteins (per serving): 40 | |
| Fats (per serving): 36 | |
| Nutritional value: ● ● ● | |

Peel and chop the onions and place half in the bottom of an oven-proof dish greased with the lard. Lay the slice of pork over them, then season with salt and pepper and cover with the rest of the onions. Moisten with the melted butter, then set in a pre-heated oven at 220°C for 30 minutes, turning the pork over half way through. When the time is up, remove from the oven, pour over the cider vinegar and a glass of water, then put back into the oven at the same temperature for another hour, basting the meat frequently with its cooking juices. In the past the *caghuse* was normally eaten cold.

# CASSOULET

Baked pork and beans ☛ *Languedoc*

1 Steep the beans for 6-8 hours in advance, then drain and tip into a large saucepan of cold water; bring it slowly to the boil and continue cooking for five minutes. Drain the beans, then tip them back into the saucepan, and cover again with warm water. Add the chopped bacon rind, the bacon, the garlic, the *bouquet garni*, the onion spiked with the cloves and a pinch of salt and pepper.

2 Cook for an hour, with the water just shivering so that the beans remain whole and firm. Melt the fat from the *confit* in a saucepan, removing the meat, and adding the chopped pork in its place with a pinch each of salt and pepper. Brown thoroughly all over, then remove and tip in the sliced sausage.

3 Take a large oven-proof dish, preferably of earthenware, and tip in almost all the beans with plenty of their liquid, along with the onion, the garlic and the *bouquet garni*. On top of this arrange a layer of the *confit* and pork, following up with the rest of the beans and finally all the remaining meat except the sausage which should be set on the top, along with the sauce from the pork saucepan. Cook in a pre-heated oven at 160°C for one hour. After this time, remove the dish and, with a fork, press down the crust which has formed on the top. Cook for a further twenty minutes and repeat the operation once or twice more.

1 kg/ 2 ¼ lb dried white beans
200 g/ 7 oz bacon rind
300 g/ 11 oz fatty bacon
4 portions of duck or goose
    preserved in their fat (confit)
    (or alternatively 2 duck thighs
    and 4-5 tablespoons of lard)
40 cm/ 16 in fresh pork sausage

750 g/ 1 ¾ lb pork
    shoulder or shin
3 cloves garlic
1 bouquet garni
1 onion spiked with 2 cloves
Salt and pepper

Servings: 8
Preparation time: 30'+6-8 h
Cooking time: about 3 hours
Difficulty: ● ● ●
Flavour: ● ● ●
Kcal (per serving): 1289
Proteins (per serving): 88
Fats (per serving): 72
Nutritional value: ● ● ●

# ENCHAUD

Pork roast in lard ☛ *Périgord and Quercy*

1 kg/ 2 ¼ lb pork fillet
3 cloves garlic
500 g/ 1 lb 2oz lard
40 g/ 1 ½ oz coarse
   or sea salt

| | |
|---|---|
| Servings: 6-8 | |
| Preparation time: 20'+ 48 h | |
| Cooking time: 2 h 30' | |
| Difficulty: ● ● | |
| Flavour: ● ● ● | |
| Kcal (per serving): 809 | |
| Proteins (per serving): 29 | |
| Fats (per serving): 74 | |
| Nutritional value: ● ● ● | |

Make a series of shallow slits in the meat and stick in small slices of garlic. Rub the fillet all over with coarse salt, then set it in a bowl, cover, and leave to rest for 48 hours.

When it is ready to cook, melt the lard in a casserole, clean the salt off the meat, dry it, and immerse in the lard. Cover the casserole, lower the heat, and cook slowly for two and a half hours.

After this place the meat in a glass or pyrex dish or bowl, and sieve the cooking fat over it, covering it completely. Seal the dish well and leave for several (6-8) weeks before eating.

# JAMBONNEAUX AU CIDRE

Pig's trotters in cider ☛*Normandy*

C lean and slice the carrots, scrape and quarter the turnips and peel the onions, leaving them whole. Place them all in a saucepan with the cider, the *bouquet garni*, the pig's trotters and sufficient salt and pepper. Cover and cook slowly for four hours, then cool and leave to rest overnight, or for a whole day. After this, replace the saucepan on the heat; remove two ladlefuls of stock and heat thoroughly in a small saucepan. Add the butter cut into flakes, and beat with an egg-whisk until you have a suitably creamy sauce, then season with salt and pepper. When the meat saucepan comes to the boil, immediately remove the trotters, divide them in half, then serve surrounded by the vegetables and with the sauce poured over.

2 pig's trotters
  of about 800 g/ 1 ³/₄ lb
  each
1 bunch round
  onions
2 carrots
2 turnips
1 bouquet garni
50 g/ 2 oz butter
1 bottle dry cider
Salt and pepper

| | |
|---|---|
| Servings: 8 | |
| Preparation time: 30'+24 h | |
| Cooking time: 4 h 15' | |
| Difficulty: ● ● | |
| Flavour: ● ● ● | |
| Kcal (per serving): 485 | |
| Proteins (per serving): 40 | |
| Fats (per serving): 22 | |
| Nutritional value: ● ● | |

# JARRET DE PORC AUX ÉPICES

Spicy pork shins ☛ *South west*

4 shins of pork
2 onions
2 carrots
2 leeks
1 tablespoon vinegar
1 tablespoon flour
1 knob butter
1 clove garlic
1 clove
1 teaspoon thyme leaves
5-6 sage leaves
1 sprig rosemary
1 bay leaf
1/4 litre/ 1/2 pint/ 1 cup
   red wine
1 teaspoon of "quatre-épices"
   (pepper, nutmeg, cloves
   and cinnamon)
   (see p. 71)
Salt and pepper

| | |
|---|---|
| Servings: 4 | |
| Preparation time: 50' | |
| Cooking time: 2 h 10' | |
| Difficulty: ● ● ● | |
| Flavour: ● ● ● | |
| Kcal (per serving): 452 | |
| Proteins (per serving): 40 | |
| Fats (per serving): 16 | |
| Nutritional value: ● ● | |

1 Set the four shins of pork in a large saucepan, cover them with cold water and add the vinegar. Boil for an hour, skimming continually, then leave to cool and remove the shins from the water. In a large casserole melt the butter and sauté the sliced leeks and carrots. Season with salt and pepper and sprinkle with flour, then cook for five minutes, stirring all the time. Add all the herbs and spices, pour over the wine and bring to the boil.

2 Put the pork shins into the casserole, making sure they are covered by the sauce, and adding a little water if there is not enough. Put the lid on the casserole, turn the heat down to minimum and cook a further 45 minutes. Pre-heat the oven to 200°C, and when the 45 minutes are up, remove the shins from the casserole, place them in a roasting-tin and cook them in the oven for about 20 minutes. While they are cooking, tip the vegetables and sauce into the blender and whiz until thoroughly creamed; adjust salt and pepper to taste and keep warm. Serve this sauce over the pork shins immediately after you remove them from the oven.

# POTÉE LORRAINE

Lorraine pottage ◆ *Lorraine*

**1** Set the beans to steep a day in advance. Next day, drain them and tip into a saucepan, cover with cold water and add one *bouquet garni*, one onion spiked with two cloves, and one clove of garlic. Bring slowly to the boil, then cover the saucepan and cook over a low heat for an hour and a half. Now prepare all the other vegetables, cleaning them and chopping roughly. Rinse all the meat under cold running water, then put it into a large saucepan, again covered with cold water. Bring to the boil and cook slowly for an hour, skimming as frequently as possible.

**2** When the hour is up, remove the meat from the saucepan, throw away the water and replace the meat along with the other spiked onion, the second *bouquet garni* and all the other vegetables except the beans and the potatoes. Cover again with cold water, season with pepper and bring to the boil. Put the lid on the saucepan, lower the heat and continue cooking for another hour and a half. Twenty minutes before the end, add the potatoes, and a quarter of an hour later, the drained beans. Finely chop the remaining clove of garlic, then blend it in with the chopped parsley and the cream. Remove the meat from the saucepan and place it on a serving dish; spoon the vegetables around it, pouring the cream, garlic and parsley sauce over them, and serve.

---

2 shins of pork
500 g/ 1 lb 2 oz fresh, slightly salted bacon
500 g/ 1 lb 2 oz pork shoulder, also slightly salted
3 fresh sausages
1 cabbage
500 g/ 1 lb 2 oz dried white beans
6 carrots
6 turnips
6 potatoes
3 leeks
1 stalk celery
2 onions, each spiked with two cloves
2 bouquet garni
2 cloves garlic
1 bunch chopped parsley
1 cup single cream
Salt and pepper

---

**Servings: 8**
**Preparation time: 40' +12 h**
**Cooking time: about 3 hours**
**Difficulty: ●●**
**Flavour: ●●●**
**Kcal (per serving): 1666**
**Proteins (per serving): 82**
**Fats (per serving): 106**
**Nutritional value: ●●●**

# POTJEVLEISCH

Mixed meat terrine ☛ *Flanders*

Wings, thighs and breast
  of 1 chicken
1 saddle of rabbit
400 g/ 14 oz veal loin
200 g/ 7 oz fresh lean bacon
100 g/ 3 ½ oz bacon fat,
  in thin slices
4 shallots
1 bottle dry white wine
2 sprigs thyme
2 bay leaves
1 tablespoon
  chopped parsley
150 g/ 5 oz bacon rind,
  in one piece
Salt and pepper

| | |
|---|---|
| Servings: 8-10 | |
| Preparation time: 30'+12 h | |
| Cooking time: 3 h 30' | |
| Difficulty: ● ● ● | |
| Flavour: ● ● | |
| Kcal (per serving): 1059 | |
| Proteins (per serving): 61 | |
| Fats (per serving): 76 | |
| Nutritional value: ● ● ● | |

1 Chop all the meat into pieces (boning the white meats if you wish). Peel and chop the shallots and mix them with the chopped parsley. Line the bottom of a deep dish with the slices of bacon fat and arrange the meat on top in alternate layers of chicken, rabbit and veal.

2 Fill up the spaces with the diced bacon and the chopped shallot and parsley mixture, and press down well so that the preparation holds together perfectly. Season with salt and pepper.

3 Sprinkle the thyme leaves and the crumbled bay leaves on top, then cover the whole with the sheet of bacon rind cut to fit the dish, and with the fat side in contact with the meat.

4 Pour over enough wine to completely cover the meat, then cover the dish, set it in a bain-marie and cook in a pre-heated oven at 160°C for three and a half hours. Leave to cool, then put in the fridge for at least 12 hours before serving.

# POULET À LA MODE DE SARE

Chicken with peppers ☞ *South west*

1 chicken
   of about 1.5 kg/ 3 ½ lb
6 ripe tomatoes
12 fresh green chilli peppers
2 red peppers
½ glass dry white wine
1 cup flour
1 onion
1 clove garlic
4 tablespoons olive oil
1 bunch parsley
3-4 sprigs thyme
Olive oil, salt and pepper

| | |
|---|---|
| Servings: 4 | |
| Preparation time: 25′ | |
| Cooking time: about 1 hour | |
| Difficulty: ●● | |
| Flavour: ●●● | |
| Kcal (per serving): 731 | |
| Proteins (per serving): 34 | |
| Fats (per serving): 39 | |
| Nutritional value: ●● | |

**1** Cut the chicken into eight pieces; season with salt and pepper and coat lightly in flour. Peel and seed the tomatoes and divide them into quarters, then do the same with the red peppers. Cut the green chilli peppers in two lengthways, clean them thoroughly and chop. Chop up the garlic and onion. Heat three tablespoons of oil in a large casserole and brown the chicken pieces, then remove them and keep warm. Pour off the fat from the casserole, and dissolve the residue in the white wine.

**2** Cook the tomatoes, peppers, garlic and onion in a large saucepan in a trickle of oil, seasoning with salt and pepper. After about ten minutes replace the chicken pieces in the casserole with the white wine, then tip in the vegetables. Sprinkle with parsley and thyme, put on the lid, and cook over a medium-low heat for 30 minutes.

# POULET AU CIDRE ET AUX CAROTTES DE CRÉANCES

Spicy chicken in cider with carrots ☛ *Normandy*

**1** Peel and quarter four of the apples and marinade them for an hour in the Calvados. Heat 30 g/ 1 oz of butter and 3 tablespoons of oil in a frying-pan and brown the chicken pieces, adding the chopped shallot half-way through, and seasoning with salt and pepper. Transfer the chicken into an ovenproof dish along with the Calvados apples, then add the cloves, the bay leaf, the thyme and the cinnamon. Pour over the cider and cook in a pre-heated oven at 180°C for 35 minutes.

**2** Meanwhile clean the carrots and boil until they are very tender. Drain them and then pass through a food-mill. Tip the purée into a small saucepan, and over a low heat blend in half the cream, a little salt and the cumin and mix thoroughly. Finally rinse and quarter the three remaining apples

without peeling them, and fry lightly in the remaining butter. Sprinkle over the sugar, and season with pepper and a pinch of the quatre-épices. Arrange the chicken in a deep dish and keep warm. Sieve the cooking juices, then heat until they are reduced by half. Add the remaining cream and cook gently for a few minutes allowing the sauce to thicken. Finally pour over the chicken, and serve with the carrot purée and the spicy fried apples.

*"Quatre-épices": this is the classic mixture of spices used in France for roast and preserved meats. It is usually made up of 5 parts of white or black peppercorns, 2 parts of nutmeg, 1 part of cloves and 2 of powdered ginger.*

1 large chicken (1.6 kg/ 3 ½ lbs) chopped into pieces
7 Golden Delicious apples
1 brimful measure of Calvados
½ litre/ 1 pint/ 2 cups sweet cider
2 cloves
½ stick cinnamon
1 bay leaf
1 sprig thyme
1 shallot
1 kg young baby carrots (preferably Crèances)
1 glass double or cooking cream
1 teaspoon powdered cumin
2 tablespoons sugar
1 pinch of "quatre-épices"
50 g/ 2 oz butter
Olive oil, salt and pepper

| | |
|---|---|
| Servings: | 4 |
| Preparation time: | 25'+1 h |
| Cooking time: | 1 h 40' |
| Difficulty: | ●● |
| Flavour: | ●●● |
| Kcal (per serving): | 1029 |
| Proteins (per serving): | 40 |
| Fats (per serving): | 48 |
| Nutritional value: | ●●● |

71

# POULET AUX OIGNONS ET FAR

Chicken with Roscoff onions and savoury batter ☞ *Brittany*

1 free-range chicken
  of about 1.5 kg/ 3 ¹/₂ lb
2-3 Roscoff or white onions
100 g/ 3 ¹/₂ oz chicken livers
200 g/ 7 oz fresh sausage
1 bouquet garni
¹/₄ litre/ ¹/₂ pint/
  1 cup milk
250 g/ 9 oz buckwheat flour
70 g/ 2 ¹/₂ oz butter
2 eggs
2 tablespoons
  chopped parsley
Salt and pepper

| | |
|---|---|
| Servings: 4 | |
| Preparation time: 20'+20' | |
| Cooking time: 1 h 15' | |
| Difficulty: ● ● ● | |
| Flavour: ● ● ● | |
| Kcal (per serving): 1248 | |
| Proteins (per serving): 69 | |
| Fats (per serving): 80 | |
| Nutritional value: ● ● ● | |

There's no doubt that Roscoff onions are a special delicacy, but if you can't find them you can use large white egg-shaped onions instead. Remove the outer skin, and if some are too big, cut them in half lengthways.

1 In a bowl, blend the flour into the eggs and milk, gradually adding a little over half a glass of water so as to obtain a batter of the kind we use for making *crêpes*. Pour into an ovenproof dish greased with 20 g/ ²/₃ oz butter and leave to rest for about twenty minutes. This is the famous Breton *far*.

2 Chop up the chicken livers small and mix them in with the sausage meat and the chopped parsley; season with salt and pepper. Stuff the chicken with this mixture then sew up the aperture. In a casserole melt the remaining butter and brown the chicken on all sides over a lively heat. Set in a roasting-tin or ovenproof dish, with the onions all around it; season with salt and pepper and add the *bouquet garni* and a glass of water. Cook in a pre-heated oven at 180°C for an hour and a quarter, basting frequently with the cooking juices. Half an hour before the cooking time is up put the *far* into the oven too. Finally serve the chicken and onions accompanied by the *far* cut into pieces.

# LES POISSONS

*From the North Sea, from the Atlantic and from the Mediterranean, from rivers, streams and lakes: dishes to make every occasion special.*

4

# RAGOÛT D'ANGUILLES ET DE CUISSES DE GRENOUILLE

Stewed eels and frogs ☛ *Loire region*

1 Boil the unpeeled garlic clove in a glass of water in a small saucepan for 10 minutes. In another small saucepan, again in a glassful of water, blanch the parsley leaves for just one minute. Remove and peel the garlic and drain the parsley, then blend both into the softened butter and set aside in a bowl.

*The countryside near Talcy.*

2 Fill a salad bowl with cold water and add the lemon juice, then plunge in the prepared artichokes (just the fleshy leaf base, discarding the tougher outer leaves and the choke) to prevent them going black. Cut into eighths and cook in a frying-pan in 20 g/ 2/3 oz butter, along with the wine and a pinch of salt.

3 Chop the eel fillets into lengths of 6 cm/ 2 1/2 in and lay them on an oven tray lined with aluminium foil, along with the frogs' legs. Melt 40 g/ 1 1/2 oz butter and brush over the eels and frogs' legs, then set in a preheated oven at 200°C for 10 minutes.

4 While you are waiting set a small saucepan on the heat and tip in the butter, garlic and parsley mixture. Add 2 tablespoons of water and the remaining butter cut into flakes; beat with an egg-whisk until the butter is thoroughly blended. When you have a smooth, creamy sauce, season with salt and pour a little into the centre of the heated individual plates. Place the frogs, eels and artichokes on top, and serve.

1 kg/ 2 1/4 lb eels, skinned, cleaned and with head and tail removed
2 artichokes
20 frogs' legs
1 clove garlic
1 bunch parsley
25 g/ 1 oz butter, softened
Juice of 1 lemon
2 tablespoons white wine
90 g/ 3 oz butter
Salt and pepper

| | |
|---|---|
| Servings: | 6 |
| Preparation time: | 20' |
| Cooking time: | 35' |
| Difficulty: | ● ● ● |
| Flavour: | ● ● ● |
| Kcal (per serving): | 876 |
| Proteins (per serving): | 43 |
| Fats (per serving): | 68 |
| Nutritional value: | ● ● ● |

# CALMARS À L'ARMORICAINE

## Squid Armorica style ☛ *Brittany*

800 g/ 1 ¾ lb squid
1 onion
2 shallots
3 cloves garlic
1 large tomato
2 tablespoons tomato
   concentrate
About 10 whole
   peppercorns, crushed
3 tablespoons cider grappa
   or cognac
1 glass dry white wine
1 glass fish stock
   (made with cube)
1 teaspoon fresh,
   chopped tarragon
1 teaspoon
   chopped parsley
Olive oil
Salt and pepper

| | |
|---|---|
| Servings: | 4 |
| Preparation time: | 25' |
| Cooking time: | 50' |
| Difficulty: | ●● |
| Flavour: | ●●● |
| Kcal (per serving): | 310 |
| Proteins (per serving): | 29 |
| Fats (per serving): | 12 |
| Nutritional value: | ● |

1 Clean the squid thoroughly, remove the skin and chop. Heat two or three tablespoons of oil in a casserole and sauté for 2 minutes over a lively heat. Add the peeled and chopped onion and shallots, the crushed garlic, the peeled, seeded and chopped tomato and the crushed peppercorns and stew for another couple of minutes, stirring all the time.

2 Pour over the grappa or cognac and set light to it; pour over the white wine and the stock and add the tomato concentrate, the parsley and the tarragon. Season with salt and mix thoroughly. Put the lid on the casserole and cook slowly for 45 minutes, then serve.

# CAUDIÈRE DE BERCK

## Northern Fishermen's soup ☞ *Boulogne region*

Scale and clean the fish, cut off the heads and tails, remove the bones and chop into chunks. Peel and slice the onions and wash and peel the potatoes, then tip them into a large saucepan with the *bouquet garni*. Add the chopped fish and pour over the wine and enough water to cover. Season with salt in moderation, and pepper. Bring to the boil, then lower the heat and cook slowly for 30 minutes. In the meantime, clean the mussels thoroughly, then open them over a lively heat for 3-4 minutes. Remove the molluscs and tip them into a warm tureen, then filter the juices.

1 Pour the mussel juices into the saucepan and, when the fish is cooked remove it with a slatted spoon and place in the tureen with the mussels. Continue cooking the rest of the soup for another 20 minutes.

2 Just before you remove it from the heat, tip in the egg yolks beaten with the cream and diluted with a few tablespoons of stock. Mix thoroughly and cook for another couple of minutes, then pour the soup over the fish. Fish out the potatoes from the bottom of the pot, set them in a bowl and serve along with the soup.

---

1.5 kg/ 3 1/2 lb saltwater fish
  (conger eel, turbot,
  John Dory)
1 kg/ 2 1/4 lb mussels
1/2 litre/ 1 pint/ 2 cups
  dry white wine
1 kg small potatoes
2 cloves garlic, 3 onions
2 egg yolks
1 glass double
  or cooking cream
1 bouquet garni (thyme,
  bay leaf and parsley)
Salt and pepper

| | |
|---|---|
| Servings: 8 | |
| Preparation time: 20' | |
| Cooking time: about 50' | |
| Difficulty: ● ● ● | |
| Flavour: ● ● ● | |
| Kcal (per serving): 637 | |
| Proteins (per serving): 56 | |
| Fats (per serving): 17 | |
| Nutritional value: ● ● | |

# CHIPIRONS FARCIS

## Stuffed squid ☞ *Pays Basque*

1.2 -1.3 kg/ 3 lb
  medium-size squid
1 onion
1 thick slice raw ham, diced
80 g bread crumb,
  steeped in milk
2 egg yolks
5 tablespoons fish stock
3 fresh green chilli peppers
3 tomatoes
2 cloves garlic
3 tablespoons Armagnac
$1/2$ teaspoon powdered
  chilli pepper
Olive oil
Salt and pepper

*For the sauce:*
2 shallots
1 clove garlic
15 tablespoons fish stock
15 tablespoons perfumed
  dry white wine
1 measure Armagnac
2 sprigs tarragon

| | |
|---|---|
| Servings: | 4 |
| Preparation time: | 30' |
| Cooking time: | 1 h 45' |
| Difficulty: | ●● |
| Flavour: | ●●● |
| Kcal (per serving): | 565 |
| Proteins (per serving): | 41 |
| Fats (per serving): | 20 |
| Nutritional value: | ●●● |

**1** Clean the squid, removing the skin and the fin, and chop up the tentacles. Peel and chop the onion and sauté in a tablespoon of oil, then add the finely chopped green chillies, the squid tentacles, the ham, the peeled, seeded and chopped tomatoes and the crushed garlic, and season with salt. Let all the tomato juice evaporate, then remove from the heat and add the stock, the squeezed bread crumb and the egg yolks. Mix all the ingredients well together, and adjust salt to taste. Stuff the squid three-quarters full with this mixture, and close the tops with a toothpick. Pour two tablespoons of oil into the bottom of an ovenproof dish, then line up the squid and cook in a pre-heated oven at 170°C for 30 minutes.

**2** While the squid are cooking, lightly sauté the chopped shallots in a tablespoon of oil, add the crushed garlic clove, pour over the wine and simmer very gently for 5 minutes. Add the stock and the chopped tarragon, cook slowly for a further 5 minutes, then tip in the Armagnac. Blend thoroughly, then pour this sauce over the squid, and return to the oven for another 30 minutes.

# DAURADE AUX CÈPES

Dorado with porcini mushrooms ☛ *Nantes region*

1 cleaned and scaled dorado
   of about 2 kg/ 4 1/2 lb
1.8-2 kg/ 4-4 1/2 lb
   porcini mushrooms
1 bunch parsley
2 cloves garlic
500 g/ 1 lb 2 oz ripe tomatoes
250 g/ 9 oz round white
   onions ("grelots")
1 green pepper
2 lemons
50 g/ 2 oz butter
1/4 litre/ 1/2 pint/ 1 cup
   dry white wine
1 sprig rosemary
1 bay leaf
Olive oil, salt and pepper

| | |
|---|---|
| **Servings: 8** | |
| **Preparation time: 20'** | |
| **Cooking time: 1 h 10'** | |
| **Difficulty:** | ● ● |
| **Flavour:** | ● ● ● |
| **Kcal (per serving): 868** | |
| **Proteins (per serving): 45** | |
| **Fats (per serving): 28** | |
| **Nutritional value:** | ● ● ● |

1 Sprinkle the inside of the fish with salt and pepper, then put in the rosemary and the bay leaf. Peel the onions, split open the pepper and remove the seeds and the white membranes, and cut into triangles. Slice the lemons and the tomatoes. Pour two tablespoons of oil into a large ovenproof dish and lay the dorado on top, covering it with the slices of lemon and the triangles of pepper. Pour over the white wine, then scatter the tomatoes and onions over the top. Season with salt and pepper and cook in a pre-heated oven at 200°C for an hour.

2 Meanwhile clean the mushrooms, cutting them up if they are too big. Chop the garlic and mix it with the chopped parsley. In a frying-pan, brown the mushrooms in the butter and 5-6 tablespoons of oil. Lower the heat, sprinkle with the garlic and parsley, season with salt and pepper and cook for about twenty minutes. When the dorado is cooked, lay on a dish, spoon the mushrooms around it, and serve immediately.

# ÉCREVISSES AU GRATIN

Crayfish gratin ☞ *Burgundy*

1 kg /2 ¼ lb freshwater
   crayfish (or, alternatively
   saltwater)
1 tablespoon coarse or sea salt
1 bouquet garni
200 g/ 7 oz single cream
1 knob butter
4 egg yolks
½ teaspoon tomato
   concentrate
1 handful spinach
Salt and pepper

| | |
|---|---|
| Servings: 4 | |
| Preparation time: 30' | |
| Cooking time: 20' | |
| Difficulty: | ● ● |
| Flavour: | ● ● |
| Kcal (per serving): 551 | |
| Proteins (per serving): 40 | |
| Fats (per serving): 38 | |
| Nutritional value: | ● ● |

**B**ring 3 litres/ 6 pints/ 12 cups of salted water to the boil, with the *bouquet garni*. Cook the crayfish for 3 minutes then drain, rinse under cold running water and peel. Sauté the spinach in the butter and keep to one side. Beat the egg yolks with the cream, the tomato concentrate, and season with salt and pepper; cook over a low heat until the sauce thickens, then pour into individual dishes, add the crayfish and the spinach and brown under the grill for a few minutes.

# HUÎTRES AU GRATIN

Oyster gratin  *Normandy*

32 fairly large oysters
80 g/ 3 oz butter
5-6 tablespoons breadcrumbs
1 glass dry cider
4 tablespoons double
  or cooking cream
Salt and pepper

| | |
|---|---|
| **Servings: 4** | |
| **Preparation time: 10'** | |
| **Cooking time: about 3'** | |
| **Difficulty:** | ● |
| **Flavour:** | ● |
| **Kcal (per serving): 418** | |
| **Proteins (per serving): 18** | |
| **Fats (per serving): 22** | |
| **Nutritional value:** | ● ● |

Open the oysters; don't throw away the water, but filter it into a cup through a fine cloth and keep aside. Take four small fire-proof dishes (of the kind used for frying eggs) and melt 20 g/ ¾ oz butter in each. Place a tablespoon of breadcrumbs in each dish and mix in until absorbed by the butter, then place eight oysters on top. Mix the filtered oyster juice with the cider and cream, and pour over the molluscs, which should be completely covered, but not floating. Season with salt and pepper, sprinkle lightly with breadcrumbs and brown in a pre-heated oven at 160°C for 3 minutes.

# LOTTE EN BOURRIDE

Angler "en bourride" ☞ *Languedoc-Roussillon*

1 angler of about 1.2 kg/ 2 lb
  10 oz
60 g/ 2 oz butter
70 g/ 2 1/2 oz fresh bacon,
  diced
2 leeks
2 small carrots
1 stalk celery
1 sprig thyme
1 bay leaf
The rind of 1/4 orange
1 onion
2 cloves garlic
1 tablespoon tomato
  concentrate
1 glass dry white wine
2 tablespoons flour
1/2 measure brandy
Olive oil
Salt and pepper

*For the "aïoli":*
4 cloves garlic
1 teaspoon tomato
  concentrate
2 egg yolks
1 teaspoon mustard
Olive oil

| | |
|---|---|
| Servings: 4 | |
| Preparation time: 30' | |
| Cooking time: 1 h | |
| Difficulty: ● ● ● | |
| Flavour: ● ● ● | |
| Kcal (per serving): 574 | |
| Proteins (per serving): 53 | |
| Fats (per serving): 29 | |
| Nutritional value: ● ● ● | |

1 In a casserole brown the angler lightly in two tablespoons of oil and 30 g/ 1 oz of butter, along with the bacon, the sliced white parts of the leeks, the sliced carrots, diced celery and finely-sliced onion, the thyme, bay-leaf, crushed garlic and orange rind. Pour over the wine, then add a scant tablespoon of tomato concentrate and a glass of water, seasoning with salt and pepper. Cook over a low heat for 35-40 minutes.

2 When the time is up, pass all the vegetables through a food-mill, and cut the angler into pieces. Coat these lightly in flour, sauté in a frying-pan in the remaining butter, pour over the brandy and set light to it, then replace the fish in the casserole along with the puréed vegetables. Cook for a further 15 minutes. Meanwhile prepare the *aïoli*. Pound the garlic in a pestle, blend in the egg yolks and gradually trickle in the oil, beating constantly. When it is thick and creamy, fold in the mustard and the tomato concentrate and add the sauce to the fish cooking juices. Pour over the fish, and serve.

# MATELOTE À L'ALSACIENNE

Alsatian fish soup ☞*Alsace*

500 g/ 1 lb 2 oz pike
500 g/ 1 lb 2 oz eels
400 g/ 14 oz tench
  or carp
400 g/ 14 oz perch
100 g/ 3 $^1/_2$ oz butter
25 g/ 1 oz onion
15 g/ $^1/_2$ oz shallot
30 g/1 oz flour
1 glass single cream
Juice of $^1/_2$ lemon
1 tablespoon cognac
$^1/_3$ litre/ $^2/_3$ pint/ 1 $^1/_3$ cups
  Alsace white wine
$^1/_4$ litre / $^1/_2$ pint/ 1 cup
  fish stock (made with cube)
200 g/ 7 oz small round onions
200 g/ 7 oz cultivated
  mushrooms
1 clove garlic
1 bouquet garni (thyme,
  parsley, bay leaf)
1 bunch parsley
Salt and pepper

**Servings: 8-10**
**Preparation time: 25'**
**Cooking time: about 40'**
**Difficulty: ● ● ●**
**Flavour: ● ●**
**Kcal (per serving): 1093**
**Proteins (per serving): 75**
**Fats (per serving): 63**
**Nutritional value: ● ● ●**

1 Chop the fish into chunks of about 50-60 g/ 2 oz, and sprinkle with salt and pepper. Heat a knob of butter in a large frying-pan and sweat the chopped onion and shallot, then tip in the fish; heat up again, pour over the cognac, the wine and the fish stock and drop in the *bouquet garni*. Cover the pan with a sheet of buttered aluminium foil, and cook slowly for about ten minutes. Peel the onions and set them in a saucepan with a pinch of salt and a knob of butter; cover with cold water then seal the saucepan with a sheet of buttered aluminium foil and cook until all the water has evaporated.

2 Bring a cupful of water with a knob of butter, a pinch of salt and a trickle of lemon juice to the boil, and steep the well-cleaned mushrooms in it for 5 minutes. Place the fish in a large casserole, laying the onions and mushrooms on top, and keep warm. Sieve the fish cooking juices, then replace in the pan and bring to the boil, reduce and bind with 40 g/ 1 $^1/_2$ oz of softened butter and 30 g/ 1 oz of flour. Beat until smooth with an egg-whisk, then gradually incorporate the cream and the juice of half a lemon. Pour the sauce over the fish, onion and mushroom dish, and heat gently for a further two minutes, then sprinkle with chopped parsley and serve.

# MORUE À LA CRÈME

*Salt cod Savoy style* ☞*Savoy*

1.2 kg/ 2 ½ lb steeped
  salt cod
3 onions
12 medium-size potatoes
Flour
Olive oil, pepper

| | |
|---|---|
| Servings: 4 | |
| Preparation time: 20' | |
| Cooking time: 20' | |
| Difficulty: ● ● | |
| Flavour: ● ● ● | |
| Kcal (per serving): 922 | |
| Proteins (per serving): 64 | |
| Fats (per serving): 43 | |
| Nutritional value: ● ● | |

1 Peel and slice the onions, brown them lightly in 3 tablespoons of oil and set aside. Boil the potatoes, peel them and cut into slices about 1 cm/ ½ in thick, then fry these too over a gentle heat in 3 tablespoons of oil.

2 Tip the onions back into the frying-pan and continue cooking for a few more minutes.

3 Wash and dry the salt cod, chop it into chunks and coat them in flour. Brown in 5-6 tablespoons of oil over a lively heat.

4 Set the fish and the vegetables in an ovenproof dish and cook in a pre-heated oven at 220°C for about ten minutes. Sprinkle generously with pepper before serving.

*The facade of the Abbey of Hautecombe, situated on the eastern shore of the Bourget lake in Savoy.*

# MORUE EN RAÏTO

Salt cod in "raïto" sauce ☞ *Provence*

800 g/ 1 ¾ lb steeped
  salt cod
4-5 ripe tomatoes
2 onions
4 cloves garlic
Capers and gherkins
Bay leaf, fennel seeds
Parsley
Sugar
Red wine
Flour
Olive oil, salt and pepper

| | |
|---|---|
| Servings: 4 | |
| Preparation time: 15′ | |
| Cooking time: about 30′ | |
| Difficulty: | ●● |
| Flavour: | ●●● |
| Kcal (per serving): 419 | |
| Proteins (per serving): 46 | |
| Fats (per serving): 12 | |
| Nutritional value: | ●● |

1 Scald the salt cod for 5 minutes, then trim and remove the skin. Wash the tomatoes, seed and chop roughly. Peel the garlic and chop it up finely with a sprig of parsley. Peel and slice the onions, then sauté them in a saucepan in 3-4 tablespoons of oil. Add the tomatoes, the chopped garlic and parsley, a pinch each of salt, pepper and sugar, one bay leaf and a pinch of fennel seeds.

2 Pour over half a glass of wine. Finely chop a scant tablespoon of capers and about a dozen small gherkins, then tip them into the saucepan and reduce over a gentle heat for about 15 minutes. Cut the cod into pieces and coat lightly in flour, then fry in 4-5 tablespoons of oil in a frying-pan. Drain and transfer to the vegetable saucepan, letting the flavours blend over a gentle heat for 5-6 minutes. Serve the cod with its sauce, garnished with lettuce leaves.

# PERCHE AUX NOIX

Perch with walnuts ☛ *Burgundy*

4 fillets of perch of about
  200 g/ 7 oz each
200 g/ 7oz fresh salted bacon
50 g/ 2 oz shelled walnuts
1 lemon
100 g/ 3 ½ oz butter
  + 1 knob
Flour
1 tablespoon chopped
  parsley
Olive oil
Salt and pepper

| | |
|---|---|
| Servings: | 4 |
| Preparation time: | 15' |
| Cooking time: | 30' |
| Difficulty: | ● ● |
| Flavour: | ● ● ● |
| Kcal (per serving): | 1001 |
| Proteins (per serving): | 36 |
| Fats (per serving): | 87 |
| Nutritional value: | ● ● ● |

1 Blanch the diced bacon for a minute, then cool and dry. Salt and pepper the fish fillets and coat lightly in flour. Heat the knob of butter and 3 tablespoons of olive oil in a large frying-pan, then cook the fish fillets on both sides over a gentle heat, basting regularly with the cooking juices. When they are cooked, sprinkle with lemon juice and keep warm.

2 Sauté the bacon in a tablespoon of oil, tip it out to dry on kitchen paper, and then put it into a clean frying-pan with 100 g/ 3 ½ oz butter; when the butter begins to foam add the walnuts and a trickle of lemon juice. Set the fish on a warmed serving dish, pour over the butter, bacon and walnut sauce piping hot, sprinkle with chopped parsley and serve with boiled potatoes.

# POULPES EN DAUBE

Octopus casserole ☞ *Provence*

1 kg/ 2 ¼ lb octopus
  (preferably small)
1 ½ onions
2 cloves garlic
1 carrot
3 ripe tomatoes
100 g/ 3 ½ oz fatty bacon
1 bouquet garni (parsley,
  thyme, bay leaf, wild fennel)
Cloves
4 glasses dry white wine
Olive oil
Salt and pepper

| | |
|---|---|
| Servings: 4 | |
| Preparation time: 25' + 3 h | |
| Cooking time: 1 h 40' | |
| Difficulty: ● ● | |
| Flavour: ● ● ● | |
| Kcal (per serving): 543 | |
| Proteins (per serving): 26 | |
| Fats (per serving): 37 | |
| Nutritional value: ● ● | |

Trim the octopus, rinsing them under cold running water, then chop them into pieces tentacles and all. Tip into a bowl, and leave to marinate for 3 hours in 4 glasses of wine, with the *bouquet garni*, salt and pepper.
Drain, keeping the marinade and the *bouquet garni* to one side. Peel the whole onion, then chop it and the scraped carrot up finely and sauté in a casserole in 4 tablespoons of oil, adding the fatty bacon cut into strips. When the bacon has coloured, tip in the peeled, seeded and chopped tomatoes and the well-drained octopus. Stir thoroughly, pour in the filtered marinade, the half-onion peeled and spiked with 3 cloves, the *bouquet garni* and the garlic. Cover and cook over a very gentle heat for an hour and a half, until the octopus is tender. Leave to cool, then warm slightly over a very gentle heat before serving.

# THON À LA PROVENÇALE

Tuna Provençal style ☞ *Provence*

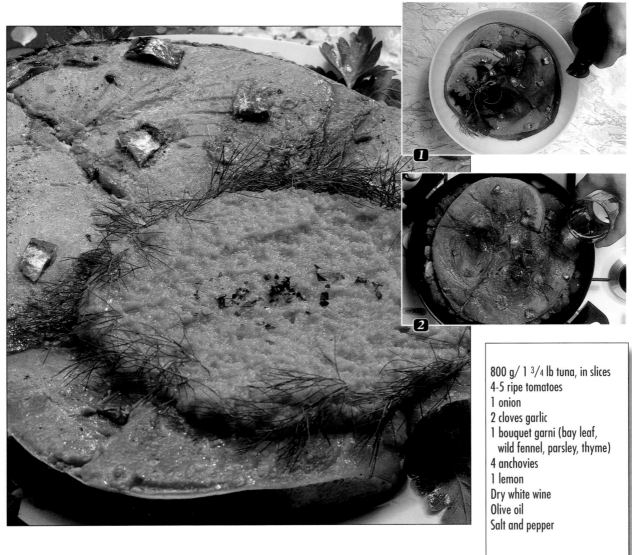

800 g/ 1 ¾ lb tuna, in slices
4-5 ripe tomatoes
1 onion
2 cloves garlic
1 bouquet garni (bay leaf,
  wild fennel, parsley, thyme)
4 anchovies
1 lemon
Dry white wine
Olive oil
Salt and pepper

| | |
|---|---|
| Servings: | 4 |
| Preparation time: | 20'+1 h |
| Cooking time: | 1 h |
| Difficulty: | ● ● |
| Flavour: | ● ● ● |
| Kcal (per serving): | 455 |
| Proteins (per serving): | 49 |
| Fats (per serving): | 19 |
| Nutritional value: | ● ● |

**1** Rinse and fillet the anchovies. Spike the tuna slices with small pieces of anchovy, then put them in a bowl with the lemon juice, the *bouquet garni* and 5-6 tablespoons of oil and leave to marinate for an hour, turning the slices over from time to time.

**2** Drain the tuna, keeping the oil to one side. Wash, seed and chop the tomatoes. Peel and finely chop the onion, then tip it into a saucepan with the marinade oil. Add the tomatoes and the crushed garlic and reduce over a very gentle heat. After about 15 minutes add the tuna, season with salt and pepper, and pour over a glass of wine. Cover and cook slowly for about 40 minutes. Serve the tuna with the sauce spooned over.

# THON BASQUAIS

Tuna with peppers ☞*Pays Basque*

800 g/ 1 ¾ lb tuna, in slices
2 onions
2 red peppers
2 green peppers
3 tomatoes
3 cloves garlic
1 dried chilli pepper
Olive oil
Salt and pepper

| | |
|---|---|
| **Servings:** 4 | |
| **Preparation time:** 15′ | |
| **Cooking time:** about 1 h | |
| **Difficulty:** ● ● | |
| **Flavour:** ● ● ● | |
| **Kcal (per serving):** 531 | |
| **Proteins (per serving):** 46 | |
| **Fats (per serving):** 31 | |
| **Nutritional value:** ● ● | |

1 Heat 5 tablespoons of oil in a frying-pan. Sprinkle the slices of tuna with salt and pepper, then colour lightly for five minutes each side. Remove from the pan and keep warm.

2 Peel and finely slice the onions, trim the green and red peppers and cut into thin strips, peel and seed the tomatoes and squeeze out the juice with a fork and slice the garlic, then tip them all into the frying-pan used for the tuna along with the chilli pepper. Season with salt and pepper and cook for ten minutes, then discard the chilli.

3 Arrange half the pepper and vegetable mixture in an ovenproof earthenware dish, then lay the slices of tuna on top.

4 Spread the rest of the vegetables over the tuna, pour over 4 or 5 tablespoons of oil, cover the dish with aluminium foil and cook in a pre-heated oven at 210°C for 30 minutes.

*The castle of Lourdes, a city set in the foothills of the central Pyrenees in south-western France, and a famous site of pilgrimage.*

# TIELLA

## Octopus pie ☞ *Languedoc*

800 g/ 1 ¾ lb baby
  octopus
4 tomatoes
1 onion
1 egg yolk
4 cloves garlic
8 stoned black olives
250 g/ 9 oz brisée pastry
  (see p. 18)
Olive oil
Butter
Salt and pepper

| | |
|---|---|
| Servings: 6 | |
| Preparation time: 25' | |
| Cooking time: about 2 h | |
| Difficulty: ●● | |
| Flavour: ●●● | |
| Kcal (per serving): 1043 | |
| Proteins (per serving): 42 | |
| Fats (per serving): 79 | |
| Nutritional value: ●●● | |

1 Bring a saucepan of water to the boil and drop the baby octopus into it, lower the heat and cook for about forty minutes.

2 Chop the onion, then sauté lightly in a casserole in two tablespoons of oil, adding the finely-chopped garlic, the peeled, seeded and chopped tomatoes, the drained octopus and the black olives. Season with salt and pepper and cook over a gentle heat for an hour.

3 Divide the pastry into two and roll out half to line the bottom of a lightly buttered flan dish or tin. Pour in the octopus filling.

4 Roll out the rest of the pastry to cover the flan-dish and seal the edges well, then brush the surface of the pastry with the beaten egg yolk. Bake in a pre-heated oven at 200°C for half an hour.

**1**

**2**

*Carcassonne: the west side of the castle.*

# TRUITES À LA MODE

Chambéry trout Savoy style ☛ *Savoy*

4 trout of about 250 g / 9 oz
   each
2 carrots
2 tomatoes
1 onion
4 cloves garlic
1 sprig thyme
1 bay leaf
1 clove
100 g / 3 ¹/₂ oz butter
1 glass dry white wine
¹/₂ glass dry white
   vermouth
Salt and pepper

| | |
|---|---|
| Servings: | 4 |
| Preparation time: | 15′ |
| Cooking time: | 20′ |
| Difficulty: | ● ● |
| Flavour: | ● ● ● |
| Kcal (per serving): | 571 |
| Proteins (per serving): | 48 |
| Fats (per serving): | 37 |
| Nutritional value: | ● ● ● |

Pour the wine and the vermouth into a large casserole, then add the diced carrots, the peeled and chopped tomatoes, the sliced onion, the chopped garlic, the thyme, bay leaf and clove. Season with salt and pepper and bring to the boil. Lower the heat and simmer the trout very gently in this stock for 12 minutes, turning them over half way through. Remove the fish and the vegetables and set them in a warmed serving dish. Sieve the cooking juices, then re-heat until they are reduced by half; add the butter, beating hard with an egg-whisk, adjust salt and pepper to taste, then pour the sauce over the trout.

# TRUITES AU RIESLING

Trout in Riesling ☛ *Alsace*

1 Use 10 g/ ⅓ oz of butter to grease an ovenproof dish, then scatter over the chopped shallots. Season with salt and pepper. Boil the mushrooms whole for 2 minutes in a small saucepan with half a glass of water, 5 g/ ⅙ oz of butter and a pinch of salt. Wash, clean and dry the trout, sprinkle them with salt and pepper, then place them on the bed of shallots. When the mushrooms are cooked, pour the cooking juices and the wine into the dish with the trout. Cover with buttered greaseproof paper, bring to the boil on the hotplate, then transfer to a pre-heated oven at 240°C for 10 minutes.

2 Once cooked remove the trout from the dish, and peel off the skin from the head downwards (see picture). Lay on a serving dish and keep warm, covered with a sheet of aluminium foil. Reduce the cooking juices until you have a syrupy consistency, then add the cream, reduce again and remove from the heat. Using an egg-whisk, beat in the remaining butter, then pour this sauce over the trout. Place a mushroom cap alongside each trout, and serve.

4 trout of about 250 g/ 9 oz each
50 g/ 2 oz butter
15 g/ ½ oz shallot
200 ml/ 6 fl oz/ ¾ cup white Riesling
1 glass single cream
4 cultivated mushroom caps of 30 g/ 1 oz each
Salt and pepper

| | |
|---|---|
| **Servings:** | 4 |
| **Preparation time:** | 30' |
| **Cooking time:** | 20' |
| **Difficulty:** | ● ● ● |
| **Flavour:** | ● ● |
| **Kcal (per serving):** | 671 |
| **Proteins (per serving):** | 46 |
| **Fats (per serving):** | 37 |
| **Nutritional value:** | ● ● ● |

# TURBOT BRAISÉ AU CIDRE

Braised turbot in cider ☛ *Normandy*

8-900 g/ about 2 lb turbot fillets
2 leeks
1 apple
150 g/ 5 oz butter
1/2 litre/ 1 pint/ 2 cups cider
1/2 litre/ 1 pint/ 2 cups fish
   stock
1/4 litre/ 1/2 pint/ 1 cup
   double or cooking cream
Salt and white pepper

| | |
|---|---|
| Servings: | 4 |
| Preparation time: | 20' |
| Cooking time: | 30' |
| Difficulty: | ● ● |
| Flavour: | ● ● |
| Kcal (per serving): | 900 |
| Proteins (per serving): | 45 |
| Fats (per serving): | 61 |
| Nutritional value: | ● ● ● |

Clean the leeks and slice them thinly, then wash and peel the apple and slice it too. Grease a low-sided ovenproof dish with 50 g/ 2 oz butter, scatter the leek and apple over the bottom then lay the turbot fillets over them. Season with salt and pepper, then slowly pour over the cider and the fish stock. Set the dish on the heat and, when the liquid begins to boil, cover with aluminium foil and transfer to a pre-heated oven at 200°C for 20 minutes, lowering the heat if it appears to be boiling too rapidly. When the time is up, remove the turbot and keep warm on a heated dish covered with aluminium foil. Filter the cooking juices into a saucepan, and whiz the solids (leeks and apple) in the blender. Heat the cooking juices until they are reduced by a third, then incorporate the remaining butter, beating constantly with an egg-whisk. Finally fold in the cream and the puréed vegetables. Heat until it is just shivering, adjust salt and pepper to taste, then pour the sauce over the turbot which should still be hot.

# LES LÉGUMES

*The flavours of the soil: vegetables and salads to accompany rich dishes, but also tasty ideas which provide the perfect inspiration for a light and appetising menu.*

5

# ARTICHAUTS À LA BARIGOULE

Artichokes "à la barigoule" ☛ *Provence*

8 artichokes
1 onion
1 carrot
2 cloves garlic
Parsley
2 slices stale bread
1 glass dry
    white wine
Olive oil
Salt and pepper

| | |
|---|---|
| **Servings:** | 4 |
| **Preparation time:** | 25' |
| **Cooking time:** | 1 h 30' |
| **Difficulty:** | ● ● |
| **Flavour:** | ● ● |
| **Kcal (per serving):** | 369 |
| **Proteins (per serving):** | 11 |
| **Fats (per serving):** | 10 |
| **Nutritional value:** | ● ● |

Trim the artichokes, removing the stalks, the tough outer leaves and the tips. Turn them upside down and press down gently on a work surface to open them out a little. Chop the garlic finely with a sprig of parsley, then blend in with the crumbled bread. Peel and chop the onion and carrot, then spread them over the bottom of an ovenproof dish and pour over 4 tablespoons of oil. Arrange the artichokes standing upright, sprinkle them with the bread, parsley and garlic mixture, garnish each with a trickle of oil and season with salt and pepper. Pour over the glass of wine, then cover the dish and cook in a pre-heated oven at 140°C for an hour and a half.

# Asperges
# à la Flamande

Flanders asparagus ☛ *Flanders*

32 asparagus
250 g/ 9 oz butter
5 eggs
1 tablespoon chopped
  parsley
Salt and pepper

| | |
|---|---|
| Servings: 4 | |
| Preparation time: 30′ | |
| Cooking time: 40′ | |
| Difficulty: ● ● | |
| Flavour: ● ● | |
| Kcal (per serving): 560 | |
| Proteins (per serving): 7 | |
| Fats (per serving): 55 | |
| Nutritional value: ● ● ● | |

Wash and peel the asparagus, then cook in salted boiling water for 30 minutes.
Hard-boil the eggs for 7 minutes, then shell them, cut four of them in half lengthways and chop the fifth. Melt the butter in a small saucepan and mix in the chopped egg. Anoint the tips of the asparagus lightly with the butter and egg mixture, then sprinkle them with the parsley and arrange eight on each plate with the two egg halves next to them. Serve the rest of the butter and egg sauce separately.

# GRATIN DE BLETTES

Spinach beet gratin ☛ *Loire region*

1 kg/ 2 ¼ lb tender spinach
  beet ribs
30 g/ 1 oz butter
20 tablespoons single cream
100 g/ 3 ½ oz soft, fresh,
  Sahnequark-type cheese
2 egg yolks
10 tablespoons double cream
  or natural yoghurt
Salt and pepper

| | |
|---|---|
| Servings: | 4 |
| Preparation time: | 20' |
| Cooking time: | 40' |
| Difficulty: | ● ● |
| Flavour: | ● ● |
| Kcal (per serving): | 481 |
| Proteins (per serving): | 11 |
| Fats (per serving): | 38 |
| Nutritional value: | ● ● ● |

*A view of the countryside
close to Montrésor.*

Wash the spinach beet thoroughly then chop into sections of 2 cm by 4 (¾ in by 1 ½). Melt the butter in a saucepan, tip in the spinach beet, cover the pan and cook over a gentle heat for 15 minutes. Pour in the single cream and continue cooking for another five minutes. Melt the soft cheese in another saucepan over a very low heat, then add to the spinach beet. In a bowl, whisk the egg yolks with the thicker cream, season with salt and pepper and add to the spinach beet mixture after you have turned off the heat. Pile the mixture in a buttered ovenproof dish and brown in a pre-heated oven at 220°C.

# HARICOTS À LA BRETONNE

Beans, Breton style ☛*Brittany*

| | |
|---|---|
| 250 g/ 9 oz fresh shelled white beans | |
| 1 bouquet garni (thyme, bay leaf, sage and parsley) | |
| 1 onion spiked with a clove | |
| 55 g/ 2 oz butter | |
| 1 onion | |
| 2 shallots | |
| 2 ripe tomatoes | |
| 1 teaspoon fresh thyme leaves | |
| Salt and pepper | |

| | |
|---|---|
| **Servings:** 4 | |
| **Preparation time:** 10' + 4-5 h | |
| **Cooking time:** 1 h 10' | |
| **Difficulty:** ● ● | |
| **Flavour:** ● ● ● | |
| **Kcal (per serving):** 256 | |
| **Proteins (per serving):** 9 | |
| **Fats (per serving):** 14 | |
| **Nutritional value:** ● ● ● | |

1 Remember to steep the beans for at least 4-5 hours before starting. After this, drain them and tip into a casserole with the *bouquet garni* and the onion spiked with a clove. Cover with cold water and cook slowly for about an hour. Drain, keeping the cooking water to one side. Season the beans with salt and pepper, and keep warm.

2 In another casserole melt the butter and sauté the chopped onion and shallots; add the peeled, seeded and diced tomatoes and cook over a very gentle heat for a couple of minutes, then add sufficient bean water to blend into a slightly creamy sauce. Pour this sauce over the beans and sprinkle with the fresh thyme.

# CHOU-FLEUR AU GRATIN

Cauliflower gratin ☛ *Île-de-France*

1 Divide the cauliflower into florets and cook them for about twenty minutes in boiling salted water. Drain and set aside.

2 Prepare a béchamel or white sauce using 50 g/ 2 oz butter, 50 g/ 2 oz flour and 2 glasses of milk. Stirring continuously over a gentle heat, towards the end pour in the cream and season with salt and pepper.

3 Remove the saucepan from the heat and incorporate 60 g/ 2 oz of Emmental cheese mixed with half the grated Parmesan. This is the famous *Mornay sauce*.

4 Butter an ovenproof dish and line up the cooked cauliflower florets, cover with the Mornay sauce, sprinkle with the remains of the two cheeses, and dot with flakes of butter. Cook in a pre-heated oven at 220°C for about ten minutes, until the surface is golden brown.

1 cauliflower of about 1.5 kg/
   3 1/2 lb
2 tablespoons lemon juice
125 g/ 4 oz butter
50 g/ 2 oz flour
2 glasses milk
1/2 glass double
   or cooking cream

80 g/ 3 oz Emmental, grated
20 g/ 2/3 oz Parmesan, grated
Salt and pepper

| | |
|---|---|
| Servings: 4-6 | |
| Preparation time: 20' | |
| Cooking time: 45' | |
| Difficulty: ● ● | |
| Flavour: ● ● | |
| Kcal (per serving): 471 | |
| Proteins (per serving): 14 | |
| Fats (per serving): 33 | |
| Nutritional value: ● ● ● | |

# POMMES DE TERRE À LA NORMANDE

Normandy potatoes ☞ *Normandy*

800 g/ 1 ³/₄ lb potatoes,
  preferably new
  and medium-sized
1 glass single cream
20 g/ ²/₃ oz butter
2 tablespoons chopped
  parsley
1 tablespoon chopped
  chervil
1 tablespoon of chopped
  tarragon
Salt and pepper

| | |
|---|---|
| Servings: 4-6 | |
| Preparation time: 30' | |
| Cooking time: 30' | |
| Difficulty: ● ● | |
| Flavour: ● ● | |
| Kcal (per serving): 352 | |
| Proteins (per serving): 6 | |
| Fats (per serving): 19 | |
| Nutritional value: ● ● ● | |

1 Boil the potatoes in salted water without peeling them and when they are cooked, drain and leave to cool slightly. Wash and dry the saucepan, then replace it on the heat and pour in the cream. Heat gently and season with salt and pepper.

2 Peel the potatoes and divide in two or leave whole (depending on size) then tip them in with the warm cream. Mix well, then add the butter cut into flakes and last of all the herbs. When all the ingredients are thoroughly mixed, remove from the heat, turn into a deep dish and serve.

# POMMES DE TERRE FARCIES

Stuffed potatoes ☞*Alsace and Lorraine*

| | |
|---|---|
| 6 large potatoes | |
| 5-600 g/1 lb 2-4 oz leftover boiled meat | |
| 125 g/ 4 oz fresh sausage | |
| 20 g/ ²/₃ oz onion | |
| 20 g/ ²/₃ oz shallot | |
| 2 tablespoons chopped parsley | |
| 2 cloves garlic | |
| Olive oil | |
| Salt and pepper | |

| | |
|---|---|
| **Servings: 6** | |
| **Preparation time: 30′** | |
| **Cooking time: 1 h 15′** | |
| **Difficulty:** ● ● | |
| **Flavour:** ● ● ● | |
| **Kcal (per serving): 645** | |
| **Proteins (per serving): 41** | |
| **Fats (per serving): 31** | |
| **Nutritional value:** ● ● ● | |

Peel the onion and shallot, wash the parsley and chop all finely; chop the meat and sausage too, then mix them all together. Peel the potatoes and halve them lengthways, then scoop out the middle taking care not to pierce the skin. Season the insides with salt and pepper, then fill them with the stuffing, levelling off at the top. Place the two halves together again and tie up with string. Heat the oil in an ovenproof dish, brown the potatoes on all sides, then set them in a pre-heated oven at 200°C for a good hour. Keep an eye on them to make sure that they do not overbrown, covering with a sheet of aluminium foil if necessary.

# POMMES SARLADAISES

Sarlat potatoes *Périgord*

1 kg/ 2 ¼ lb waxy
   potatoes
100 g/ 3 ½ oz goose fat
   or lard
3 cloves garlic
1 bunch parsley
Salt and pepper

| | |
|---|---|
| Servings: | 6 |
| Preparation time: | 20' |
| Cooking time: | 30' |
| Difficulty: | ● |
| Flavour: | ● ● ● |
| Kcal (per serving): | 449 |
| Proteins (per serving): | 6 |
| Fats (per serving): | 26 |
| Nutritional value: | ● ● ● |

Peel the potatoes and cut into three or four pieces. Chop the parsley and garlic. In a large saucepan melt half the fat and brown the potatoes lightly over a rapid heat for 10 minutes, turning them frequently. Cover the pan and cook for a further quarter of an hour, stirring regularly, then break them up into smaller pieces with a fork. Add the rest of the fat, season with salt and pepper and add the chopped garlic and parsley, then cook for a further 10 minutes until they are nice and crispy. Serve piping hot.

# RATATOUILLE NIÇOISE

Nice ratatouille — *Nice region*

**P**eel and slice the aubergine. Lay the slices on a dish, sprinkle with sea salt and lay a weight on top so that the bitter juices run off. Peel and slice the onion. Wash the tomatoes, then seed and dice them. Clean and trim the zucchini, and dice them without peeling. Trim the peppers, removing the seeds and white membranes, then cut into thin strips. Drain, rinse and dry the aubergine slices, then dice them. Tip all the vegetables into a large saucepan with two tablespoons of oil, the *bouquet garni* and the garlic; season with salt and pepper and simmer for 30 minutes. The classic *ratatouille*, a traditional vegetable dish, is excellent both hot and cold. It can be served on its own (with couscous or bulgher) or as an accompaniment to meat and fish dishes.

2 onions
2 peppers
2 zucchini
5 ripe tomatoes
4-5 cloves garlic
1 aubergine
1 bouquet garni (bay leaf,
  basil, parsley, time,
  wild fennel)
Olive oil
Salt and pepper

| | |
|---|---|
| Servings: 4 | |
| Preparation time: 25'+10' | |
| Cooking time: 30' | |
| Difficulty: ● ● | |
| Flavour: ● ● ● | |
| Kcal (per serving): 156 | |
| Proteins (per serving): 3 | |
| Fats (per serving): 10 | |
| Nutritional value: ● ● | |

# SALADIER LYONNAIS

Lyons salad ☞ *Lyons region*

1 sheep's trotter, already
   boiled
3 hard-boiled eggs
2 chicken livers, singed rapidly
   in a trickle of oil
2 marinated herring fillets
A few sprigs of dill and chives,
   chopped

*For the vinaigrette:*
5 tablespoons olive oil
1 tablespoon mustard
1 tablespoon vinegar
Salt and pepper

| | |
|---|---|
| Servings: 4 | |
| Preparation time: 15' | |
| Difficulty: ● | |
| Flavour: ● ● ● | |
| Kcal (per serving): 461 | |
| Proteins (per serving): 47 | |
| Fats (per serving): 29 | |
| Nutritional value: ● ● | |

Dice the sheep's trotter, chop the chicken livers, slice the hard-boiled eggs, and cut the herrings into chunks; tip all into a salad bowl, then sprinkle with the dill and chives. In a bowl blend the *vinaigrette* ingredients, then pour over the salad.

# LES DESSERTS

*Irresistible temptations,
from Picardy to Languedoc:
the fitting finish to a special occasion, or to give
a touch of flair to a simple meal.*

6

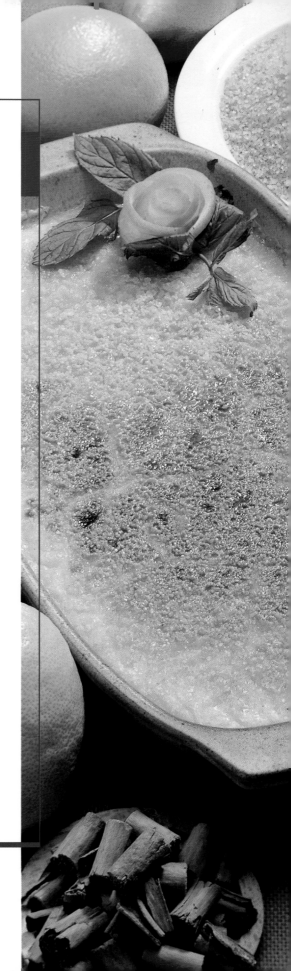

# BOURDELOTS

Apple dumplings ☛ *Normandy*

250 g/ 9 oz puff pastry
4 medium-sized apples
Juice of 1 lemon
1 egg yolk
4 tablespoons sugar
4 tablespoons red
   fruit jelly

| | |
|---|---|
| Servings: 4 | |
| Preparation time: 20′ | |
| Cooking time: 30′ | |
| Difficulty: ● | |
| Kcal (per serving): 600 | |
| Proteins (per serving): 6 | |
| Fats (per serving): 32 | |
| Nutritional value: ● ● ● | |

Roll out the pastry and cut out 4 squares of 20 cm/8 in each. Peel and core the apples, moisten with lemon juice and sprinkle with sugar. Very carefully place one apple in the centre of each pastry square, then bring the corners together at the top to make four parcels, sealing the edges carefully by moistening them with water. Brush with egg-yolk and bake in a pre-heated oven at 180°C for half an hour, lowering the temperature if they become too brown. Remove from the oven, make a small hole in the top of each package and pour in the fruit jelly.

*The islet of Mont-Saint-Michel.*

# CAJASSÉ DE SARLAT

Sarlat tart ☛ *Périgord*

250 g/ 9 oz flour
125 g/ 4 oz sugar
¹/₂ litre/ 1 pint/ 2 cups
  warm milk
A pinch of salt
3 eggs
2 tablespoons rum
3 tablespoons double
  or cooking cream

| | |
|---|---|
| **Servings:** 4-6 | |
| **Preparation time:** 15′ | |
| **Cooking time:** 30′ | |
| **Difficulty:** ● ● | |
| **Kcal (per serving):** 707 | |
| **Proteins (per serving):** 18 | |
| **Fats (per serving):** 15 | |
| **Nutritional value:** ● ● ● | |

In a deep bowl, mix the flour with the sugar and salt, then make a well in the centre and break in the eggs. Begin to beat with an egg-whisk, trickling the milk in gradually, followed by the rum and the cream. Mix thoroughly until you have a very smooth cream, then pour this into a fairly deep porcelain ovenproof dish. Bake in a pre-heated oven at 240°C for 15 minutes, then lower the temperature to 200°C and cook for a further 15 minutes. Serve the cake warm.

# CREMA CREMADA

Crème brûlée ☞ *Roussillon*

1 litre/ 2 pints/ 4 cups milk
2 eggs and 5 yolks
100 g/ 3 ½ oz granulated
  sugar
50 g/ 2 oz Demerara sugar
25 g/ 1 oz flour
25 g/ 1 oz cornflour
1 piece cinnamon bark
1 vanilla stick
Peel of 1 lemon
Peel of 1 orange
1 teaspoon of green aniseed
  (optional)

| | |
|---|---|
| Servings: 4 | |
| Preparation time: 25' | |
| Cooking time: 30' | |
| Difficulty: ● ● ● | |
| Kcal (per serving): 555 | |
| Proteins (per serving): 28 | |
| Fats (per serving): 24 | |
| Nutritional value: ● ● ● | |

1 Pour the milk into a saucepan, bring to the boil then remove from the heat. Add all the flavourings, cover and leave to cool. This should preferably be done a day in advance.

*The fertile countryside around Carcassonne, in Languedoc-Roussillon.*

2 Using a hand or electric whisk, beat together the yolks and the whole eggs, the granulated sugar, the flour and the cornflour, until you have a thick white slightly foamy mixture. Sieve the flavoured milk, and incorporate delicately into the egg mixture.

**3** Pour into a casserole, set over a very gentle heat and stir with a wooden spoon until the cream thickens. Let it boil for one minute then remove from the heat and beat energetically.

**4** Pour into an earthenware ovenproof dish and leave to cool, then put in the fridge. When you are ready to serve, sprinkle the Demerara sugar over the top and set under the grill for 3 minutes to caramelise. Serve immediately with the top piping hot and the custard cold, this contrast being the characteristic feature of the pudding.

3 eggs
¹/₄ litre/ ¹/₂ pint/
 1 cup milk
60 g/ 2 oz sugar
90 g/ 3 oz flour
300 g/ 11 oz stoned
 dried prunes
A few drops vanilla essence
1 tablespoon Calvados
30 g/ 1 oz butter

| | |
|---|---|
| Servings: | 4 |
| Preparation time: | 15′+10′ |
| Cooking time: | 40′ |
| Difficulty: | ● ● |
| Kcal (per serving): | 453 |
| Proteins (per serving): | 13 |
| Fats (per serving): | 16 |
| Nutritional value: | ● ● ● |

# FAR AUX PRUNEAUX

Prune "far" or batter pudding ☛ *Brittany*

*A young Breton woman in traditional costume.*

Beat the eggs with the sugar in a bowl until they are white and frothy. Beating all the time, add the flour, the vanilla essence and the Calvados.
Pre-heat the oven to 250°C and set the buttered cake tin in it for a few minutes so that the butter melts and turns a pale hazel colour. Pour the batter into the hot tin and scatter the prunes over the top. Bake at 250°C for 10 minutes, then lower the heat to 180°C and cook for a further 25 minutes. If the pudding should become too brown on top, cover with a sheet of aluminium foil.

# KOUIGN-AMAN

Sugar and butter pastry ☛ *Brittany*

**1** In a large bowl, mix the flour with the salt and the baking powder. Make a well in the centre and pour in 20 g/ 2/3 oz melted butter and a scant glass of water. Blend the ingredients into a smooth paste, then roll into a ball and leave to rest for half an hour wrapped in a damp tea-cloth.

Roll out the pastry into a small square 1 cm/ 1/2 in high, then dice 225 g/ 8 oz of butter into 1 cm/ 1/2 in cubes and scatter them over it. Fold the four corners in to the centre, covering all the butter, then set aside in a cool place for 15 minutes.

**2** Roll out again into a rectangle three times the size of the original square, then fold in three to form a square again. Wrap in the damp tea-cloth and leave to rest for an hour in a cool place. Finally roll the pastry out again in a long rectangle, sprinkle with sugar and fold in three once again, then leave to rest in a cool place for a further 30 minutes. Meanwhile butter a baking-tray and dust it with flour; roll out the pastry a last time into a regular shape, lay on the baking-tray and bake in a pre-heated oven at 210°C for 30 minutes.

250 g/ 9 oz butter
275 g/ 10 oz flour
225 g/ 8 oz granulated
  sugar
6 g/ 1/4 oz salt
6 g/ 1/4 oz baking powder

| | |
|---|---|
| Servings: 6 | |
| Preparation time: 45' + 1h 30' | |
| Cooking time: 30' | |
| Difficulty: ● ● ● | |
| Kcal (per serving): 915 | |
| Proteins (per serving): 7 | |
| Fats (per serving): 54 | |
| Nutritional value: ● ● ● | |

# KOUGELHOPF

Almond cake ☞*Alsace*

1 Flake the yeast into a bowl, pour over a glass of warm milk and half the flour, and work until you have a firm dough. Roll into a ball and leave to rise until it has doubled in size.

2 Tip the remaining flour into another bowl along with the salt, the beaten eggs and the other glass of warm milk. Knead for a quarter of an hour, then incorporate 250 g/ 9 oz softened butter, the sugar and the ball of leavened dough. Knead well together, then cover with a damp tea-cloth and leave to rest for an hour.

3 In the meantime, steep the raisins in the kirsch; when the dough is ready, roll it out, then dent it here and there and stick in the raisins.

4 Take a special *kougelhopf* cake tin (a special type of fluted mould like those used for puddings), butter it well, sprinkle the bottom and sides with the almonds, then fill with the dough up to the rim. Leave to rest for another hour, then bake in a pre-heated oven at 180°C for 45 minutes. If it should brown too quickly, cover the top with a sheet of aluminium foil.

25 g/ 1 oz fresh yeast
2 glasses milk
1 kg/ 2 ¼ lb flour
15 g/ ½ oz salt
3 eggs
300 g/ 11 oz butter
150 g/ 5 oz sugar

150 g/ 5 oz raisins
1 measure kirsch
75 g/ 3 oz flaked almonds

| | |
|---|---|
| Servings: 4 | |
| Preparation time: 30'+3 h | |
| Cooking time: 45' | |
| Difficulty: ● ● ● | |
| Kcal (per serving): 1403 | |
| Proteins (per serving): 27 | |
| Fats (per serving): 58 | |
| Nutritional value: ● ● ● | |

# MATEFAIM AUX POMMES

Apple "matefaim" ☞ *Lyons region*

50 g/ 2 oz flour
A pinch baking powder
1 kg/ 2 ¼ lb renette apples
50 g/ 2oz raisins
50 g/ 2 oz sugar + 1 teaspoon
1 measure rum
1 egg
2 small glasses milk
50 g/ 2 oz butter
1 teaspoon salt

| | |
|---|---|
| Servings: 4 | |
| Preparation time: 40'+2 h | |
| Cooking time: 30' | |
| Difficulty: ●● | |
| Kcal (per serving): 660 | |
| Proteins (per serving): 6 | |
| Fats (per serving): 14 | |
| Nutritional value: ●●● | |

1 Put the raisins in a cup with the rum and leave them to macerate for at least an hour. Peel, trim and core the apples and cut into 1 cm/¹/₂ in slices. Heat a frying-pan and cook the apples in 20 g/ ²/₃ oz of butter, then pour over the sugar and caramelise. Add the raisins and remove from the heat.

2 Dissolve the baking powder in the warm (not over 30°C) milk, then add the egg yolk, the flour, the salt and the teaspoon of sugar. Mix thoroughly, then set aside for at least an hour at room temperature. Beat the egg-white until it is stiff, then fold into the paste along with the apples and raisins. Heat the remaining butter in a non-stick frying-pan, tip in the batter and cook over a low heat for 4-5 minutes each side.

# MILHASSOU

Maize meal pudding ☛ *South west*

1 litre/ 2 pints/ 8 cups milk
250 g/ 9 oz maize meal
250 g/ 9 oz butter
1 tablespoon orange flower
   water
8 eggs
250 g/ 9 oz icing sugar

| | |
|---|---|
| **Servings:** 4-6 | |
| **Preparation time:** 30′ | |
| **Cooking time:** 40′ | |
| **Difficulty:** ● ● | |
| **Kcal (per serving):** 1363 | |
| **Proteins (per serving):** 36 | |
| **Fats (per serving):** 82 | |
| **Nutritional value:** ● ● ● | |

1 Boil the milk in a large saucepan, remove from the heat and sprinkle in the maize meal. Stir constantly and energetically until the mixture is tepid, then beat in 200 g/ 7 oz butter cut into flakes and add the orange flower water.

2 Beat the eggs, then mix them gradually into the batter, continuing to stir uninterruptedly for 10 min-utes. Finally tip in the sugar and blend it in thoroughly. Butter an ovenproof dish, pour in the batter and bake in a pre-heated oven at 160°C for 35-40 minutes.

# PIQUEUCHÂGNE

Baked candied apples
*Burgundy and Champagne*

8 apples
100 g/ 3 ½ oz honey
1 bunch Muscatel grapes
50 g/ 2 oz icing sugar
1 egg

*For the cream:*
50 g/ 2 oz liquid honey
3 egg yolks
100 g/ 3 ½ oz thick cream
1 lemon

*For the pastry:*
250 g/9 oz flour
1/4 litre/ ½ pint/ 1 cup milk
10 g/ ⅓ oz baking powder
100 g/ 3 ½ oz butter
1 egg
A pinch of salt

| | |
|---|---|
| Servings: 8 | |
| Preparation time: 1 h 20′ | |
| Cooking time: 1 h | |
| Difficulty: ● ● ● | |
| Kcal (per serving): 1375 | |
| Proteins (per serving): 23 | |
| Fats (per serving): 44 | |
| Nutritional value: ● ● ● | |

1 Wash and core the apples, then slice off the tops and set aside. Line the apples up in a non-stick baking tin, cover with honey and bake in a pre-heated oven at 80°C for an hour to candy them. Leave to cool.

2 Dissolve the baking powder in the warm milk, then whiz in the blender for 3 minutes along with the flour, the egg, the salt and the butter cut into flakes.

3 Divide the pastry into eight pieces and roll each out into a strip ½ cm/ ¼ in thick, 3 cm/ 1 ¼ in wide and 10 cm/ 4 in long. Keep in a warm place.

4 To prepare the cream, warm the honey in a saucepan. Grate the rind of the lemon, squeeze the juice and mix both in a bowl with the cream and the egg yolks. Tip into the saucepan along with the honey and cook slowly for a few minutes. Spread this paste over the pastry strips, wrap them around the base of each apple, then brush them with the beaten egg. Butter an ovenproof dish, and line up the apples in it. Put one grape inside each apple, then re-place the top. Sprinkle with icing-sugar and bake in a pre-heated oven at 150 °C for an hour.

*A view of Gevrey-Chambertin in Burgundy.*

# SAINT-HONORÉ

*Île-de-France*

| | |
|---|---|
| 250 g/ 9 oz fresh or frozen puff pastry | |
| 400 g/ 14 oz whipping cream | |
| 50 g/ 2 oz chopped hazelnuts | |
| 15 g/ ¹/₂ oz cocoa powder | |
| 30 g/ 1 oz icing sugar | |

*For the choux pastry:*
4 eggs; 100 g/ 3 ¹/₂ oz butter; 100 g/ 3 ¹/₂ oz flour; 100 ml/ 3 ¹/₂ fl oz/ ¹/₂ cup milk; Salt; Icing sugar

*For the confectioner's custard:*
4 egg yolks; 90 g/ 3 oz flour; 80 g/ 2 ³/₄ oz sugar; 350 ml/ 10 fl oz/ 1 ¹/₄ cups milk; Vanilla essence; 30 g/ 1 oz butter

*For the chocolate glacé icing:*
1 egg white; 30 g/ 1 oz icing sugar; 25 g/ 1 oz cocoa powder

| | |
|---|---|
| **Servings:** | 6 |
| **Preparation time:** | 1h15'+2 h |
| **Cooking time:** | 1h |
| **Difficulty:** | ● ● ● |
| **Kcal (per serving):** | 1370 |
| **Proteins (per serving):** | 20 |
| **Fats (per serving):** | 96 |
| **Nutritional value:** | ● ● ● |

Roll out the puff pastry and cut out a circle to fit the base of the cake tin (use a 28 cm/12 in diameter spring-form tin with a removable base, and line it with greaseproof paper). Lay the pastry in the tin and prick it all over with a fork. Put the choux pastry in a piping bag with a smooth nozzle (1 cm/ ¹/₂ in diameter) and pipe a ring of balls at a distance of 1 cm/¹/₂ in from the edge, and then another ring inside it. Use the remaining choux pastry to pipe about 10 balls of a diameter of about 1.5-2 cm/1 in on a baking-tray lined with greaseproof paper. Place both the cake tin and the baking-tray in a pre-heated oven at 180°C and bake for 30 minutes, making sure that they do not over-brown, then remove and leave to cool. Prepare the chocolate glacé: beat the egg-white with the icing sugar until stiff, then gradually incorporate the cocoa diluted in a drop of warm water. Spoon about half the confectioner's custard into the piping bag, attach a long, narrow nozzle, and fill all the choux balls. After this dip the balls from the baking-tray into the chocolate glacé. Whip the cream, keeping about a quarter aside for decoration. Prepare the chantilly by folding the icing sugar and the remaining confectioner's custard into the whipped cream with the egg-whisk. Spoon the chantilly cream into the cake base, covering the choux pastry balls, then sift over a layer of cocoa powder. Set the chocolate-coated choux balls at intervals around the edge, then pipe whirls of whipped cream in between them using the piping bag with a fluted nozzle. Carefully remove the Saint-Honoré from the tin, decorate the sides with the chopped hazelnuts, and keep in the fridge for a couple of hours before serving.

*To make the choux pastry, put the butter in a small saucepan with a teaspoon of sugar, the milk and a drop of water, and let it melt slowly over a gentle heat. Gradually add the flour and a pinch of salt, and stir until smooth. Beat in the eggs one at a time, until you have a dense and glossy paste.*

*To prepare the confectioner's custard, pour the milk into a small saucepan, add a drop of vanilla essence, and bring slowly to the boil. Beat the egg yolks with the sugar in a bowl, then gradually stir in the flour. Pour in the boiling milk, stirring with the egg-whisk, then tip the mixture back into the saucepan. Bring to the boil, beating all the time, then allow to thicken for about 10 minutes. Remove from the heat and leave to cool.*

# TARTE À L'BADRÉE

Milk and cream cake ☞ *Picardy*

Beat the egg yolks and the whole egg with the sugar until they are white and frothy. Bring the milk just to boiling point, then pour it over the cream and the vanilla-flavoured icing sugar in a bowl and mix in thoroughly. Roll out the pastry and use it to line a buttered 24 cm/ 10 in cake-tin. Mix together the egg and the milk mixtures, then pour into the pastry case, filling it right up to the brim. Scatter over about twenty dried prunes, previously steeped in the rum, then bake in a pre-heated oven at 210°C for 35 minutes.

250 g/ 9 oz fresh or frozen
   puff pastry
1/2 litre/ 1 pint/ 2 cups milk
1 egg + 7 yolks
120 g/ 4 oz sugar
3 tablespoons thick double
   or cooking cream
2 sachets vanilla-flavoured
   icing sugar
A knob of butter
20 dried prunes, stoned
4 tablespoons rum

Servings: 6
Preparation time: 35'
Cooking time: 40'
Difficulty: ● ●
Kcal (per serving): 798
Proteins (per serving): 23
Fats (per serving): 47
Nutritional value: ● ● ●

# TARTE SOLOGNATE AUX ÉPICES

Spicy apple tart ☞ *Sologne*

1 kg/ 2 ¼ lb
  renette apples
125 g/ 4 oz softened butter
75 g/ 3 oz sugar
1 flat teaspoon
  of powdered, nutmeg,
  cinnamon and liquorice
  mixed
100 g/ 3 ½ oz puff pastry

*For the sweet spicy sauce:*
1 untreated lemon
¼ litre/ ½ pint/ 1 cup
  apple juice
1 tablespoon acacia honey
50 g/ 2 oz butter
½ flat teaspoon
  of powdered nutmeg,
  cinnamon and liquorice
  mixed

| | |
|---|---|
| Servings: 6 | |
| Preparation time: 35' | |
| Cooking time: 1 h | |
| Difficulty: ● ● ● | |
| Kcal (per serving): 782 | |
| Proteins (per serving): 3 | |
| Fats (per serving): 48 | |
| Nutritional value: ● ● ● | |

*The castle of Chambord in the Loire valley,
 in the department of Loir-et-Cher,
 a masterpiece of Renaissance architecture.*

1 First of all prepare the sauce. Grate the lemon rind (making sure you remove only the yellow part) then squeeze the juice into a saucepan and add the apple juice, the grated rind, the honey and the butter. Bring to the boil, then simmer gently for 2 minutes. Remove from the heat and sprinkle in the half teaspoon of sweet spices. Set aside, leaving the flavours to blend while you prepare the cake.

2 Peel the apples, then halve, core and quarter them. Take a heavy-bottomed or copper tin with a diameter of about 16 cm/ 6 ½ in and 5 cm/ 2 in deep, and spread the bottom evenly with the softened butter. Sprinkle with sugar then arrange the apple quarters in it, pressing them down lightly so that they adhere perfectly to the butter.

other 10 minutes until the pastry is lightly browned. Leave to cool slightly, then turn the cake out by placing a plate over the top and turning it over quickly. Pour over the spicy sauce and serve.

3 Set the tin over a low heat, and begin cooking, removing from the heat as soon as the butter and sugar turn a nice golden colour. Transfer to a pre-heated oven at 170°C and bake for 40 minutes.

4 In the meantime roll the puff pastry into a circle of about 20 cm/ 8 in. When the apples are cooked, remove from the oven, cover with the pastry and return to the oven for an-

1 kg/ 2 1/4 lb renette
  or Golden Delicious apples
100 g/ 3 1/2 oz butter
120 g/ 4 oz sugar
30 g/ 1 oz vanilla-flavoured
  icing sugar
200 g/ 7 oz puff pastry

| | |
|---|---|
| Servings: 6 | |
| Preparation time: 35' | |
| Cooking time: 1 h | |
| Difficulty: ● ● ● | |
| Kcal (per serving): 507 | |
| Proteins (per serving): 4 | |
| Fats (per serving): 20 | |
| Nutritional value: ● ● ● | |

# Tarte Tatin

"Tatin" apple tart ☞*Sologne*

Choose an ovenproof porcelain flan dish of a diameter of about 22 cm/ 9 in. Place over a very low heat and melt the butter slowly; add the two types of sugar and mix thoroughly. Peel, core and wash the apples, then slice not too thinly and arrange them in the flan dish in a concentric pattern. Replace the dish over a low heat for 20-25 minutes, stirring with care and making sure that the caramel turns gold without becoming brown. Remove from the heat and leave to cool. Roll the pastry out to a thickness of about 2 mm/ 1/ 10 in and cut out a circle larger than the flan dish. Place over the apples, pressing the pastry down between the apples and around the edge. Bake in a pre-heated oven at 220°C for 15 minutes, then lower the temperature to 170°C and continue cooking for another 20 minutes. Turn out the cake onto a plate while it is still warm, and serve.

# TEURGOULE

Rice pudding 🖙 *Normandy*

Pour the rice into a deep earthenware dish, add the salt and the cinnamon and mix well, then pour in the milk and add the sugar. Continue stirring very gently, then set the dish in a pre-heated oven at 120°C and cook for between 4 and 5 hours (the cooking time depends on the type of oven, in a fan-heated oven 4 hours will be sufficient). A sort of brown crust should form on the top of the pudding which serves to keep the rice soft and moist, and for this reason it is essential that the pudding should never be stirred while it is cooking. One cooked, the *teurgoule* should be served at room temperature.

2 litres/ 4 pints/ 8 cups fresh
   unpasteurised full cream milk
200 g/ 7 oz round grain
   (pudding) rice
200 g/ 7 oz sugar
1 teaspoon of powdered
   cinnamon
A pinch of salt

| | |
|---|---|
| Servings: | 6 |
| Preparation time: | 10' |
| Cooking time: | 5 h |
| Difficulty: | ● ● |
| Kcal (per serving): | 464 |
| Proteins (per serving): | 13 |
| Fats (per serving): | 13 |
| Nutritional value: | ● ● ● |

*The original recipe for this traditional pudding calls for unpasteurised milk, of the kind used to make the famous Camembert cheese; nevertheless the result is superb even when ordinary pasteurised milk is used.*

127